The Christian Entrepreneur Series: **31 Steps to Purposeful Planning:**
for Christian Entrepreneurs who desire to
Achieve Extraordinary Levels of Success Worth Celebrating

PURPOSEFUL PLANNING:

for Christian Entrepreneurs
who desire to
Achieve Extraordinary Levels of Success
Worth Celebrating

The Christian Entrepreneur Series

by
Dr. Karen Lindwall-Bourg

President of the National Association of Christian Women Entrepreneurs ©
and
Karen Bourg Companies ©

Purposeful Planning by Karen Lindwall-Bourg @ **KAREN BOURG COMPANIES** © 2020

COPYRIGHT ©

DEDICATED TO

Courtenay Collins

You have been my right arm, second thinking cap, soundboard, artistic designer, and so much more since 2012!

Thank you!

WHAT PEOPLE ARE SAYING

Purposeful Planning by Karen Lindwall-Bourg is exactly as it is titled—a "purposeful planning system for Christian Entrepreneurs who desire to achieve extraordinary levels of success worth celebrating." I am thrilled that Karen has complied all of this into a book. In completing the 31 steps outlined in *Purposeful Planning*, I now have a plan of action that I know I can complete and achieve success.

Part One: "Prepare to Plan" encompasses much more than just deciding to plan; I have thoroughly prayed and planned for my vision, purpose, values, and dreams. The step-by-step process has enabled me to begin with the right mindset—and then to pick my goal, plot my course of action, and put measures in place to evaluate and motivate me in seeing my plan completed.

Part Two: Through "Plan Purposefully," daily, weekly, monthly, and quarterly best practices have been initiated for my unique plan.

Part Three: "Progress Along the Plan Path" has guided me in setting up action and tracking worksheets which are great motivators for me to stay the course and experience success daily. Additionally, issues that tend to derail my progress have already been addressed, enabling me to spot them quickly and make changes necessary to keep on track.

An essential conclusion to *Purposeful Planning* is Part Four, "Praises." Perspective is placed on why I have planned. Success in reaching my goals is why I have planned so diligently. Therefore, I also have a plan to celebrate, rest, rejuvenate, and play in anticipation of

Part Five: "Plan Again." I will utilize the Purposeful Planning book again and again!

Angela S. Hallford
http://furthermoreliving.com

Last December I joined the first Purposeful Planning group. I set aside a day to plan and organize because I felt like my business and life had way too many steps jumbled together to know what to do. The brain dump and organization were done in one BIG day. Creating that plan was one of the greatest aspects of 2019! I then decided to do a marathon and spent 24 hours completing my Purposeful Plan over about four days. The focused energy of designing that plan and executing it made it possible to more than exceed my goals. My "Ta-Done list" included fixing my website and creating content for it; getting my seven journals in print; revising two short books; and creating covers, blogs, and power pages for my business. I am forever grateful for Karen's Purposeful Planning Program!

Danika Deva
www.DanikaDeva.com

ACKNOWLEDGEMENTS

Who taught you to plan well?

I'm grateful to every Life and Business Coach I've had since 2012 because each one of them has taught me to plan well. I can't wait to see what future coaches teach me!

Betty Richardson of Richardson, TX – you walked me through my first, second, and third (I think) comprehensive Non-Profit Strategic Plan all in one day's work. What a Day! I really think that was when the "entrepreneur dream" first sprouted for me. I wanted to be you! And as the Program Director, then Client Services Director, then Board of Directors member of those three organizations, I used the Strategic Plan as a virtual bible. In each case, it expertly guided me through every process and task before me!

Diane Cunningham Ellis – you taught me to plan with brave visions and dreams as my guide through my early entrepreneur endeavors. And you taught me to plan retreat style. I am hooked on travel meetings now!

Elayna Fernandez – you taught me to plan based on my passions and to blog about it along the way.

Kadena Tate – you taught me to plan strategically and according to Business Canvases/Patterns that have worked wonders!

Shelley Hitz – you taught me to plan intensely and completely in one sitting. You also introduced me to the Pomodoro technique, which has practically become a daily ritual—a lifestyle!

Alex Fletcher – you taught me to plan each night for the next day and each week for the next week. What a relief each morning and the beginning of each week is now!

Kim Smith – you taught me to plan on a budget, with wisdom; and you taught me to see money through or from God's view!

Angela Hallford – you taught me to plan based on my God-given T.A.L.E.N.T.S. – Temperaments, Ambitions, Leadership Style, Experiences, Needs, Talents, and Spiritual Gifts!

Thank you to every National Association of Christian Women Entrepreneur friend and member (http://nacwe.org) and Karen Bourg Companies follower and client (http://karenbourg.com) – you have inspired me to seek Him and to BE more like Christ in my life and work PLANS every day!

Thank you Lee Desmond, Managing Director of RHEMA Publishing House (http://rhemapublishinghouse.com) – couldn't and wouldn't want to edit and publish without you!

Thank you, dear husband Fred, and all our "Bourg Bunch" Blended Kids and "Grandorables" – you deserve credit for blending us well and for honoring Tim and Cathy along the way!

Thank YOU, Jesus Christ, My Savior – You received even me.

TABLE OF CONTENTS

INTRODUCTION

Welcome to *Purposeful Planning: Steps for Christian Entrepreneurs* (Book 1 in *The Christian Entrepreneur Series*)!

It's my greatest desire that through this process and these tasks of planning well, you will achieve extraordinary levels of success worth celebrating.

Let's celebrate together!

I am a former medical technologist, trained to be organized, productive, exact, and analytical so that medical professionals' work and patients' lives are enhanced.

I am a Licensed Professional Counselor, Family Therapy Ph.D., and Biblical Counselor trained to listen well, assess, analyze with wisdom, and lead counselees to seek and hear the Lord for direction for their current struggles.

I am a life and entrepreneur coach who has fallen in love with the processes and tasks required to grow and manage my own business in ways that please the Lord. I love seeing others grow and their borders expanded—this is what now makes my "world go 'round!"

If I've learned anything from my coaches (see acknowledgments), I've learned that I won't succeed without a plan, and the plan must be purposeful. Entrepreneurship can be lonely, which is why there are so many like-minded entrepreneur communities online. And events and circumstances change moment to moment; so, we must be proactive instead of reactive to serve the Lord well.

I am not alone!
You are not alone!

Let's Purposefully Plan together!

Blessings,
Karen

WHAT TO EXPECT

On Your Own

You can work through this workbook or follow along in this recorded course on your own, if you desire. Take your time. Pray your way through. Ask questions if you get stuck. Use the Worksheets at the back of the book if you want to see your great progress in one concise place.

In a Group

I find I make much better progress if I work through these steps in one day and with others (at least virtually) beside me.
To join us for a Planning DAY, contact Karen at karen@karenbourg.com .

For more information:
http://karenbourg.com/PlanDesignFollowThrough

If you join us for Plan, Design, Follow Through [PDF2] MASTERMIND Series you'll be invited to this great group:
https://www.facebook.com/groups/PlanDesignFollowThrough/

From Karen, the Author

As a reader, writing coach, and Shepherding publisher, I'm frustrated when writers don't use correct spelling and grammar. When I write for myself and my own online programs, I break a lot of rules on purpose and for emphases. If you're a reader like me, I apologize in advance. If you're a writer like me, let me know – I'm feeling a bit alone out here!

From Karen, the Speaker

On stage, I speak from the heart, but online I can't afford to chase down a rabbit trail or my courses will fail. You'll see me follow notes very closely to keep us on task and on time.

From Karen, the Coach

There is no greater joy than to walk alongside another entrepreneur and grow together! Seeing you succeed thrills me. It's my "WHY" and the reason I cannot NOT do this! I insist on having a discovery call with every potential client so we both know with certainty that I am the best servant leader/coach for you. I coach in 12-week packages/increments, and you'll see why as you work through this book. Let's ***achieve extraordinary levels of success worth celebrating*** together!

Amen!

JOIN

I invite you to join me in NACWE (http://nacwe.org) [http://facebook.com/groups/NACWEFreedom] and Karen Bourg Companies (http://karenbourg.com) as we continue to plan together well in years to come.

For help Implementing your Plans,
– In small groups, join our Elite Membership and/or our Mastermind Group http://nacwe.org/join
– For expert Individual Coaching, Planning Retreats and VIP Sessions, join Karen https://karenbourg.com/work-with-me/. Working with me includes FREE Access to groups above.

PDF Special – Take a look at http://NACWE.Org/join/
for "4" easy payment options and all of the benefits included!

Our Schedule

1st Quarter [**PDF²**]
January – PLAN
February – Design A-Z – Marketing, etc.
    Writing Retreat
March – Follow Through

2nd Quarter [**PDF²**]
April – PLAN
    Writing Retreat
May – Design A-Z – Marketing, etc.
June – Follow Through

3rd Quarter [**PDF²**]
July – PLAN
    Writing Retreat
August – Design A-Z – Marketing, etc.
September – Follow Through
    NACWE Conference

4th Quarter [**PDF²**]
October – PLAN
November – Design A-Z – Marketing, etc.
    Writing Retreat
December – Follow Through

But First:
PREPARE TO PREPARE!

Literally DREAM ABUNDANT ideas for your goals for the next 12-weeks, within all dimensions of your life, from your heart and soul, onto a large poster board. Fill it up!

You will add to and tweak this list along the Purposeful Planning Path, so feel free to be creative with it.

Consider:
What abundance are you asking God for as you plan these next 12-weeks?

Try a quick assessment of your strengths and challenges in the following areas. Avoid negativity, Celebrate Successes, AND ASK GOD FOR ABUNDANCE in each area.

Using the acrostic B.E.L.I.E.F.S. ask yourself what you'd like to accomplish in each area:

• **BODY**/Physical Wellness _____

• **Emotional** Wellness _____

• **LIVELIHOOD**/Occupational Wellness_____

    • _____

    • _____

    • _____

    • _____

    • _____

    • _____

• **Intellectual** Wellness _____

• **Environmental** Wellness _____

• **FAMILY/FRIENDS**/Social Wellness _____

• **Spiritual** Wellness _____

Now, align your Dream Poster and this list, then go back and **ADD even more abundantly** to your dream list!

We will refer to this growing list often at the beginning of the Purposeful Planning Way. You'll add to it more than once. Then you'll use it to clarify and F.O.C.U.S. (Follow One Course Until Successful) as you plan.

"A dream written down with a date becomes a goal. A goal broken down into steps becomes a plan. A plan backed by action makes your dreams come true." Greg Reid, *Wealth Made Easy*

Our hope is that you will Dream BIGGER with the Lord and ask Him for abundance in all areas of your life and work. For more information about our use of the B.E.L.I.E.F.S Assessment, see the book *WELLNESS: The Awareness of the Whole Individual* on Amazon at https://t.ly/1nOWB or https://www.amazon.com/Karen-Lindwall-Bourg

JOURNAL: FROM *MY SOUL THIRSTS FOR THE LIVING GOD*

I don't know about you, but I thirst after God—I long to know His thoughts, I desperately want to follow His Purposeful Plan. I have to intentionally remember

- to invite Him to remind me of my Identity and the Calling He has placed on my life as a Christian Woman Entrepreneur
- to invite Him into every Purposeful Plan, big or small
- to invite Him into the Design of every Marketing Program I create for each Plan
- to invite Him into the Launch, the Ask, the Conversations, the relationships.

And, I often invite Him in, ask for His Guidance, and then run off on some frenzied tangent before He has even begun to speak to me. No wonder the thirst and longing and desperation continues, and I am frequently frustrated in my entrepreneur endeavors!

SO, I invite you to invite Him into every step of the Purposeful Planning Pathway set before you. Please don't dive in until you have quietly sat before Him and until you have truly heard Him speak. Journal your thoughts along the way.

Start with PRAYER!

READ Psalm 42 English Standard Version (ESV) **Bold is mine.** Highlights are mine. Record any keywords that speak to you!

Why Are You Cast Down, O My Soul?
To the choirmaster. A Maskil of the Sons of Korah.

1 ***As a deer pants for flowing streams, so pants my soul for You, O God.*** **2** *My soul thirsts for God, for the living God. When shall I come and appear before God?*	_____ _____ _____ _____

3

*My tears have been my food
day and night, while they
say to me all the day long,
"Where is your God?"*

4

*These things I remember,
as I pour out my soul:
how I would go with the throng
and lead them in procession
to the house of God
with glad shouts and
songs of praise,
a multitude keeping festival.*

5

*Why are you cast down,
O my soul, and why are you
in turmoil within me?*
**Hope in God; for I shall again
praise him, my salvation
6 and my God.**
*My soul is cast down within me;
therefore **I remember you**
from the land of Jordan
and of Hermon,
from Mount Mizar.*

7

*Deep calls to deep
at the roar of your waterfalls;
all your breakers and your
waves have gone over me.*

8

**By day the Lord commands
his steadfast love, and
at night his song is with me,
a prayer to the God of my life.**

9

I say to God, my rock:
*"Why have you forgotten me?
Why do I go mourning
because of the oppression
of the enemy?"*

10 *As with a deadly wound in my bones, my adversaries taunt me, while they say to me all the day long, "Where is your God?"* *11* *Why are you cast down, O my soul, and why are you in turmoil within me?* **Hope in God; for I shall again praise him, my salvation and my God.**	_____ _____ _____ _____ _____

English Standard Version (ESV)
The Holy Bible, English Standard Version. ESV® Text Edition: 2016. Copyright © 2001 by Crossway Bibles, a publishing ministry of Good News Publishers.

You might want to also read it in The Passion Translation for added emphasis. Psalm 42 The Passion Translation (TPT) **Bold is mine.** Highlights are mine.

Book 2
The Exodus Psalms

Psalms of suffering and redemption
A Cry for Revival[a]

42 *For the Pure and Shining One*
A contemplative poem for instruction, by the prophetic singers of Korah's clan[b]
"As the deer pants for the riverbank [water's edge],"
[1] I long to drink of you, O God,
drinking deeply from the streams of pleasure
flowing from your presence.
My longings overwhelm me for more of you![c]
The literal Hebrew is "as the deer pants for the riverbank [water's edge]." *This translation takes the metaphor of a hunted deer and puts it into terms that transfer the meaning into today's context. David is describing the passion and longing he has that is yet unfulfilled.*
[2] My soul thirsts, pants, and longs for the living God.
I want to come and see the face of God.
[3] Day and night my tears keep falling
and my heart keeps crying for your help

while my enemies mock me over and over, saying,
"Where is this God of yours? *Why doesn't he help you?*"
⁴ So I speak over my heartbroken soul,
"Take courage. Remember when you used to be
right out front leading the procession of praise
when the great crowd of worshipers
gathered to go into the presence of the Lord?
You shouted with joy as the sound of passionate celebration
filled the air and the joyous multitude of lovers
honored the festival of the Lord!"
⁵ So then, my soul, why would you be depressed?
Why would you sink into despair?
Just keep hoping and waiting on God, your Savior.
For no matter what, I will still sing with praise,
for living before his face is my saving grace!
⁶ Here I am depressed and downcast.
Yet I will still remember you as I ponder the place
where your glory streams down from the mighty mountaintops, lofty and
majestic—*the mountains of your awesome presence.*[d]
⁷ My deep need calls out to the deep kindness of your love.
Your waterfall of weeping sent waves of sorrow
over my soul, carrying me away,
cascading over me like a thundering cataract.
⁸ Yet all day long God's promises of love pour over me.
Through the night I sing his songs,
for my prayer to God has become my life.
⁹ I will say to God, **"You are my mountain of strength**;
how could you forget me?
Why must I suffer this vile oppression of my enemies—
these heartless tormentors who are out to kill me?"
¹⁰ Their wounding words pierce my heart
over and over while they say,
"Where is this God of yours?"
¹¹ So I say to my soul,
"Don't be discouraged. Don't be disturbed.
For I know my God will break through for me."
Then I'll have plenty of **reasons to praise him all over again.**
Yes, **living before his face is my saving grace!**

Think of a time when you longed for God as if your soul were panting after God "as the deer pants for flowing streams."

_____

_____

_____

_____

_____

_____

_____

Then follow this guided journal process and receive God's Blessing. Walk through this process for every dimension of wellness in the BELIEFS system above. Walk through this process asking God to lead you to your next business/ministry plan with confidence. Walk through this process focused on the PLAN you want to complete during the next quarter.

I, and my fellow entrepreneurs, have never walked away empty handed.

JOURNAL Pages

PREPARATION:

Spend a moment quietly before the LORD.

Breathe in for ___ seconds: out for ___.

Listen to Praise & Worship music:

He is NEAR:

What is the Name of your Purposeful Plan?

Remember a time when God was with you as you dreamed and planned.

Express gratitude for His presence.

What is HIS Response to your gratitude?

Ask the LORD a question about your Pending PLAN!

What is the pressing issue you need to bring before the Lord today?

In addition to this issue, is there anything else (to **get to the root issue**)?

_____

How is this Pending PLAN Question making you feel?

This is how I think/feel this issue is affecting me.

_____

_____

_____

_____

_____

_____

_____

_____

_____

_____

_____

_____

_____

_____

_____

_____

What will the future hold if nothing changes [to **see the high cost of doing nothing**]?

The RESPONSES of GOD – HE has HOPES and plans for improving your future.

What has the LORD promised in this area? (ADD Scripture as often as you can.)

_____

Thank Him for HIS Promises.

Listen and record His words as HE says, "I know this is a big deal for you!"

"I hear you_____

I see you _____

I can help you _____

I want _____ for you!"

Your Desires

What's the most powerful thing you can ask God for? *"Cast thy burden upon the Lord, and he shall sustain thee"* (Psalm 55:22).

Tell the Loving Lord what you want/desire.

What does the preferable future look like to you? How does this desire align with His Will and His Word?

_____

_____

_____

_____

_____

_____

_____

_____

_____

_____

_____

_____

_____

_____

_____

_____

Write this: He *"is able to do **far more abundantly than all that we ask or think**, according to the **power at work within us**..."* *(Ephesians 3:20)*

Your Responsibilities

Based on God's response, what's the one thing you cannot fail to do, the one basic action that will affect change, make a difference if you do it with consistency and excellence?

Practical Steps toward that ONE action I feel called to take as I LISTEN to and RESPOND to GOD! These are the things you can do, activities you can plan out, highly leveraged steps that produce great results to make your objectives happen.

a. _____

b. _____

c. _____

(F.O.C.U.S. = Follow One Course Until Successful). What will it take now to F.O.C.U.S. on the God-given task before you? Put it on your calendar, then P.A.C.T. Plan, take Action, Commit, & Track your progress.

_____

_____

_____

_____

_____

_____

_____

_____

_____

_____

_____

_____

_____

_____

_____

PART I

PREPARE TO PLAN

1

PREPARE TO PRAY AND PRAY TO PREPARE

I'm learning that you should

- prepare to pray first of all, and that you should
- pray as you prepare to serve the Lord in your business/ministry.

PREPARE TO PRAY

It's important when you prepare to pray that you fill your hearts and minds with the goodness of God. Use Isaiah's prayer in chapters 63 & 64 as an example. He says, "I will recount the steadfast love of the Lord, the praises of the Lord, according to all that the Lord has granted us, and the great goodness to the house of Israel that He has granted them according to His compassion, according to the abundance of His steadfast love." Isaiah prepares to pray by *filling his mind with the goodness of God.*

How do you prepare to pray? _____

Consider journaling your preparation to pray here. _____

_____

_____

_____

_____

_____

PRAY AS YOU PREPARE

Then, you should pray as you prepare to do what God has called you to do. Tasha Glover, one of the Kingdom Driven Entrepreneur Mentors, once said, "Invite God into every process or task before you start!" I love that! It took my breath away! It's a great reminder. I'm trying to remember and commit to inviting HIM in every day, every moment! Let's start by inviting Him into our prayer and into our preparation to plan. We want to hear from Him as we seek clarity of purpose for the day, the week, the month, and the year. We are asking Him for peace for the future and anointing for our offers.

What process or task do you need to invite God into today as you plan this new/current offer?

_____

PRAY

Pray for Wisdom.

"If any of you lacks wisdom, let him ask God, who gives generously to all without reproach, and it will be given him. 6 But let him ask in faith, with no doubting,..." James 1:5-6a

What is your primary goal for this planning session and this dated time frame of planning?

_____

_____

Journal your prayer here; be willing to ask Him for wisdom and ask Him to bless your plans in faith and without doubt!

_____

_____

_____

_____

_____

_____

AND You'll hear me ask this question often.
Is there something you need to **ADD** to your Dream list?

Step 1 as you PLAN PURPOSEFULLY is PREPARE TO PRAY & PRAY TO PREPARE. Tell us how we can pray for you.

Read this BLOG. Please leave a comment for us to tell us what you've learned. https://nacwe.org/2014/10/06/waiting-out-the-storm/

2

GATHER NEEDED TOOLS—YOU HAVE EVERYTHING YOU NEED

Before you begin, you may be wondering what tools you will need and even if you have all that you need to plan well and perform well. Let me assure you, you DO!

God Provides

First, you have all you need to live a life that is godly, that brings God glory, to share in His promises and more. Read this reminder of His Calling on your life and your work. [**Bold** and **underline** mine.]

> [3] His divine power has **granted to us all things** that pertain to life and godliness, through the knowledge of him who called us to[c] his own glory and excellence, [4] by which he has granted to us his precious and very great promises, so that through them you may become partakers of the divine nature, having escaped from the corruption that is in the world because of sinful desire. [5] For this very reason, make every effort to supplement your faith with virtue, and virtue with knowledge, [6] and knowledge with self-control, and self-control with steadfastness, and steadfastness with godliness, [7] and godliness with brotherly affection, and brotherly affection with love. [8] For if these qualities[f] are yours and are increasing, they keep you from being <u>ineffective or unfruitful</u> in the knowledge of our Lord Jesus Christ. [9] For whoever lacks these qualities is so nearsighted that he is blind, having forgotten that he was cleansed from his former sins. [10] Therefore, brothers,[g] be all the more diligent to confirm your calling and election, for if you practice these qualities you will never fall. [11] For in this way there will be richly provided for you an entrance into the eternal kingdom of our Lord and Savior Jesus Christ.
> [12] Therefore I intend always to remind you of these qualities, though you know them and are established in the truth that you have. [13] I think it right, as long as I am in this body, to stir you up

*by way of reminder, [14] since I know that the putting off of my
body will be soon, as our Lord Jesus Christ made clear to me. [15]
And I will make every effort so that after my departure you may
be able at any time to recall these things.* 2 Peter 1

Write an affirmation to remind yourself that God has given you all you need.

_____

_____

_____

_____

_____

Tools and Resources

Now, gather all the tools and resources you need to plan well.

Make this process your own; this is only a guide.

Decide on the scope of your plan—not yearly, but quarterly, monthly,
weekly, daily...

In the National Association of Christian Women Entrepreneurs, we read
through Brian Moran and Michael Lennington's book, "The 12-Week Year:
Get More Done in 12 Weeks than Others Do in 12 Months." They suggest that
annual plans include pitfalls and lead to low productivity. Planning in 12-week
increments leads to focus and clarity and urgency so you get more done and
experience improved and profound results.

Yes, we plan generally for 12-18 months in advance, sometimes more, but on
this Purposeful Planning Path, we now focus on 12-week segments of time and
have been so much more successful.

Gather Your Tools. Perhaps these include:

• Calendar – Record important dates already on your calendar.
• Planners
• Blank Notebooks
• Pencils, Pens, Markers – of varying colors
• Sticky notes

- What's on your LIST?

  - _____
  - _____
  - _____
  - _____
  - _____
  - _____
  - _____

Have fun, write by hand as often as you can, use color, and be creative!

Step 2 as you PLAN PURPOSEFULLY is to GATHER NEEDED TOOLS!

Read this BLOG. Please leave a comment for us to tell us what you've learned. https://nacwe.org/2014/12/19/five-free-tools/

3

RECALL AND CELEBRATE THE MANY WAYS GOD HAS HELPED YOU PREPARE AND GUIDED YOU TO PLAN IN THE PAST

Express Gratitude for every milestone.

Celebrate each one.

Have FUN—Think outside the box and allow yourself to BE CREATIVE and artistic!

Keep a file of encouraging tidbits you received throughout the year, or a daily gratitude calendar, and re-visit it often.

Write a thank you note to someone who encouraged you this past year.

Check out the 5-Minute Journal APP process. Here are its elements:

In the MORNING:
Save an image!

– Write out your favorite quote.
– Write 3 things you are grateful for.
– What will you do to make today great?
– Daily Affirmations – Write, "I am..."

In the EVENING:

– Write 3 Amazing things that happened today.
– How could you have made today even better?

Is there something you need to **ADD** to your Dream list?

Step 3 as you PLAN PURPOSEFULLY is to Recall and Celebrate the Many Ways God Has Helped You Prepare and Guided You to Plan in the Past.

JOURNAL:

Write out your favorite quote.

_____

_____

_____

Write 3 things you are grateful for.

_____

_____

_____

What will you do to make today great?

_____

_____

Daily Affirmations – Write, "I am…"

_____

_____

Write 3 Amazing things that happened today.

_____

_____

_____

How could you have made today even better?

_____

_____

_____

Read these BLOGs. Please leave a comment for us to tell us what you've learned.
https://nacwe.org/2015/04/28/wellness-for-women-entrepreneurs/
https://nacwe.org/2011/11/13/seven-unique-ways-to-make-a-gratitude-journal-you-can-stick-with/

4

DEFINE YOUR "WHY"

Do you know "WHY" you do what you do?

What really drives you?
What's the first desire you have when you awaken each morning and consider your day?
What would you do even if you didn't reap a reward of any kind (fame, money, etc.) for it?
What makes you smile?

My "Why" is to help Christian Entrepreneurs achieve extraordinary levels of success worth celebrating. When they smile, I smile! When they succeed, I succeed! When I celebrate, I teach them to celebrate!

Can you describe WHY you do what you do without telling us what you do?

_____

_____

_____

_____

_____

_____

_____

_____

_____

_____

_____

_____

Watch "Know Your Why | Michael Jr." at https://www.youtube.com/watch?v=1ytFB8TrkTo

He said, "People know that I do comedy, but that's WHAT I do. My "WHY" is to inspire people to walk in purpose!"

After watching his video, what are 3 things that would make you "sing" like Mr. Duff did?

1. _____

2. _____

3. _____

Step 4 as you PLAN PURPOSEFULLY is to Define Your "WHY."

Post your "WHY" and one link to what you do in our FREE Group under the "Marketplace Monday" meme on Facebook at http://facebook.com/groups/NACWEFreedom where we provide community, networking, education and missions opportunities for you.

Read this BLOG. Please leave a comment for us to tell us what you've learned. https://nacwe.org/2011/09/20/building-a-foundation-for-purpose-2/

5

CHOOSE CHARACTER AND CORE VALUES FOR YOUR ORGANIZATION AND FOR THIS PLAN

Character comes first.

But the Lord said to Samuel, *"Do not look on his appearance or on the height of his stature, because I have rejected him. For the Lord sees not as man sees: man looks on the outward appearance, but the Lord looks on the heart."* 1 Samuel 16:7

Examine your heart before the Lord, as His servant, as a worker, and as a leader.

Choose Core Values

Choose Core Values—for your organization, for your 90-day goals, and for your projects and tasks.

Core values are what drive your business and your life. It is likely you already have a set of core values associated with your life and business/ministry.

In the National Association of Christian Women Entrepreneurs (NACWE at http://nacwe.org), we hope our Character includes

- **N**urturing
- **A**dding Value to ALL we encounter
- **C**oncern & Love for everyone
- **W**orship
- **E**ncouragement

Our Core Values are

- **COMMUNITY** – in which we create and instill **Connection, Collaboration,** & **Contribution.**

- **NETWORKING** through which we value **Nurture** in relationships & **Newness** through innovative offers.
- **EDUCATION** by which we value **Empowerment, Encouragement, Excellence, & Expressiveness.**
- **MISSIONS** through which we value **Ministry** & Making a difference by Paying-it-Forward.

Actions Speak Louder than Words

You may already have adopted core values and actions such as excellent customer service or always writing a personal note to a potential customer. These actions are part of your core values. As Entrepreneurs who want to further the Kingdom as you do what God has called you to do, you are called to a higher standard—character, service, and values that align with His Word so everyone you touch will be drawn toward a more intimate relationship with Him.

Take a minute to think about what you have been called to accomplish. How do you want your customers or clients to feel? How do you want to feel about your clients? What will you never do? What will you always do? What motivates you to keep going in your business?

Ask the Lord for direction.

BONUS ENTREPRENEUR ENDEAVOR (EE) TIP: Add these to your "About" section on your website and social media sites.

Share your most important character focus and core values in the comments below. You never know who you might inspire or be inspired by! Need help? Let's talk about it.

CHARACTER

_____

_____

_____

_____

_____

_____

_____

CORE VALUES

_____

_____

_____

_____

_____

_____

_____

Is there something you need to **ADD** to your Dream list?

Step 5 as you PLAN PURPOSEFULLY is to CHOOSE CHARACTER and CORE VALUES for Your Organization/for this PLAN.

Read this BLOG. Please leave a comment for us to tell us what you've learned.

https://nacwe.org/2012/08/22/how-being-a-christian-entrepreneur-affects-my-business/
What are Chari's Core Values?

6

SET STRATEGIC STATEMENTS

6a

YOUR MISSION: SHOULD YOU CHOOSE TO ACCEPT IT!

Creating Your Mission & Vision Statement:

Part 1

YOUR MISSION: Should You Choose to Accept it!

What patterns emerged from your Dream list?

What character qualities and core values define YOU and your business/ministry?

These should influence your mission and vision statements, and vice versa!

Your mission statement focuses on today and what your organization does. I would add, your mission statement communicates your "Why."

Your vision statement focuses on tomorrow and what the organization wants to become and how you plan to grow. Some often use mission and vision statements interchangeably; I encourage you to have both.

One doesn't work without the other, because having purpose and meaning are critical for any business.

A mission statement is a short statement of why your business exists, your overall goal, and identifies the goal of your operations (wikipedia.com). It is a **brief** statement that describes the purpose or goal of a business or organization.

Your mission statement communicates the passion behind what you do—the core of your entrepreneur endeavors—and from it come your objectives and what it takes to reach those objectives. It also shapes the culture of YOU and your business/ministry.

From it may come your Organization's TAG LINE—even shorter, more concise.

To enhance your mission statement, ask questions like:

- WHY do I do what I do?
- What do I do?
- Whom do I serve?
- How do I serve them?

A solid mission motivates you and your team to advance toward a common goal.

Examples:

Facebook

Mission: To give people the power to build **community** and bring the world **closer** together.

Vision: People use Facebook to stay connected with friends and family, to **discover** what's going on in the world, and to **share** and **express** what matters to them.

(**Bold** = mine.)

What I like about it: Facebook's mission is focused on the community their platform promises. Their vision talks about <u>why</u> community matters, interweaving <u>how</u> they will "bring the world closer together" from the mission.

Uber

Mission: Uber's mission is to bring **transportation** – for everyone, everywhere.

Vision: <u>**Smarter transportation**</u> with fewer cars and greater access. Transportation that's <u>safer, cheaper, and more reliable</u>; transportation that creates more <u>job opportunities and higher incomes</u> for drivers.

(**Bold** & <u>underline</u> = mine.)

What I like about it: Uber "transports," so it is the perfect actionable verb for their mission. The vision dives deeper into how their transportation services exist for the greater good of everyone.

Share your Mission Statement with us:

_____

_____

_____

_____

_____

_____

_____

Does a TAG Line emerge that empowers your clients? It's not about you; it's all about them. Make them the hero!

_____

_____

Next, you'll write out your Vision. Borrow and bring forward some key words or phrases from your Mission Statement above.

_____

_____

_____

_____

_____

_____

_____

Step 6 as you PLAN PURPOSEFULLY is Creating Your Mission & Vision Statement—YOUR MISSION Statement.

Read this BLOG. Please leave a comment for us to tell us what you've learned. Daren Martin, author of _A Company of Owners_, suggests a company "Mantra" as opposed to Mission Statement.
https://nacwe.org/2016/12/05/book-review-company-owners/
What do you think?

Footnote:
BONUS: because the Lord just gave me this as I wrote!
You might have a personal statement:
(Core Values – Faith-filled & Faith-full, Service, Gratefulness)
[Mission – to bring glory & honor to the Lord]
{Vision – to work as unto the Lord by prayerfully and intentionally inviting Him in to every process or task before me.}

Tag Line: Honor the Lord with Me

Steps

- Be STILL, Listen
- Read 1 Timothy 1:17
- Read Colossians 3:23-24
- Study 2 Timothy 2:15
- Grow & be Equipped 2 Timothy 3:16-17

- _____

6

SET STRATEGIC STATEMENTS

6b

BE EXTRAORDINARILY VISIONARY ABOUT YOUR VISION

Create Your Mission & Vision Statement:

Part 2

YOUR VISION: Be Extraordinarily Visionary About your Vision

Remember: Your mission statement focuses on today and what your organization does and defines your WHY for others.

Envision Your Vision!!!

Vision Statement

"And the Lord answered me: "Write the vision; make it plain on tablets, so he may run who reads it. For still the vision awaits its appointed time; it hastens to the end—it will not lie. If it seems slow, wait for it; it will surely come; it will not delay." Habakkuk 2:2-3

Your vision statement focuses on tomorrow and what the organization wants to become. Some commonly use mission and vision statements interchangeably; I encourage you to have both. One doesn't work without the other, because having purpose and meaning are critical for any business.

A vision statement is a road map, indicating what your business/ministry wants to become by setting a defined direction for your growth (wikipedia.com). I would add that it explains or at least hints at *how* you will fulfill your mission.

Your vision statement communicates aspiration and gives you direction.

It is the future of your business, which then fulfills your purpose.

The vision statement is about what your business/ministry wants to become *in the future.* **It is aspirational!**

To develop a sound vision statement, ask yourself these questions:

- Who and what are you inspiring to change?
- What problem are you solving, and what pain are you relieving for your ideal client?
- How will you help solve these problems? What solutions do you offer and what glory will be experienced in the outcome?
- What are your hopes and dreams for the future?

Think like your client and answer these questions.

Put yourself in his or her shoes and answer these questions.

If all else fails, answer these questions from your own viewpoint as you sought to create or join this company.

The vision statement promotes growth, both internally and externally. A strong vision helps you and your team focus on what matters most for your company. It also invites innovation. A purpose-driven company envisions success as a whole because you know what success means for your company.

We would love to hear about your mission and vision.

Share your Extraordinary Visionary Vision Statement with us:

_____

_____

_____

_____

_____

Is there something you need to **ADD** to your Dream list?

Step 6b as you PLAN PURPOSEFULLY is to Be Extraordinarily Visionary About Your Vision.

Read this BLOG. Please leave a comment for us and return here to tell us what you've learned.
https://nacwe.org/2011/08/05/ask-diane-what-is-a-vision-statement/
https://nacwe.org/2014/09/02/7-tips-create-vision-forward-momentum/

7

DREAM MORE ABUNDANTLY THAN YOU NORMALLY ASK OR THINK, BECAUSE GOD IS...

When Cindy Burger of HolyListening.com introduced our group to the Breath Prayer, she asked us to Breath IN a Name of God, and then Breath OUT, "I want _____."

I caught my breath and was hesitant to say to our loving God "who is able to do far more abundantly than all that we ask or think," what I wanted. I needed to be reminded that He is able, and I can ask! He cares what I want!

Write this down: *"He is able to do **far more abundantly than all I ask or think**, according to His **power at work within me."*** (Ephesians 3:20, ESV)

_____

_____

_____

_____

_____

_____

_____

Read the following Scriptures:

Prayer for Spiritual Strength

*"14 For this reason I bow my knees before the Father, 15 from whom every family[c] in heaven and on earth is named, 16 that according to the riches of His glory He may grant you to be **strengthened with power** through His Spirit **in your inner being**, 17 so that **Christ may dwell in your hearts through faith**—that you, being **rooted and grounded in***

*love, [18] may **have strength to comprehend with all the saints what is the breadth and length and height and depth**, [19] and to **know the love of Christ that surpasses knowledge**, that you may **be filled with all the fullness of God.***
*[20] Now to Him who is able to do **far more abundantly than all that we ask or think**, according to the **power at work within us**, [21] to Him be glory in the church and in Christ Jesus throughout all generations, forever and ever. Amen."*
Ephesians 3, ESV

(**Bold** = mine.)

What abundance are you asking God for as you plan these next 12-weeks?

Try a quick assessment of your strengths and challenges in the following areas. Avoid Negativity, Celebrate Successes, AND ASK GOD FOR ABUNDANCE in each area.

B.E.L.I.E.F.S.

–**BODY**/Physical Wellness _____

–**Emotional** Wellness _____

–**LIVELIHOOD**/Occupational Wellness _____

- _____
- _____
- _____
- _____
- _____
- _____
- _____

–**Intellectual** Wellness _____

–**Environmental** Wellness _____

–**FAMILY/FRIENDS** = Social Wellness _____

–**Spiritual** Wellness_____

Now, go back and **ADD even more abundantly** to your Dream list!

Our hope is that you will Dream BIGGER with the Lord and ask Him for abundance in all areas of your life and work!

Step 7 as you PLAN PURPOSEFULLY is to DREAM MORE ABUNDANTLY THAN YOU NORMALLY ASK OR THINK, BECAUSE of WHO GOD IS.

Read this BLOG. Please leave a comment for us to tell us what you've learned.
https://nacwe.org/2012/03/29/courage-to-follow-your-dreams/
https://nacwe.org/2011/11/02/live-your-dreams/

8

MAKE A LIST AND CHECK IT TWICE!

Add to Your DREAM List

Spend significant time on this step!

Make a list of all the things you want to accomplish in the next 12 weeks to 90 days. I said, "check it twice," but instead of "check it twice," I really want you to **add to it twice – at least**! NACWE Sisters worked through the book *The 12-Week Year: Get More Done in 12 Weeks than Others Do in 12 Months* by Brian Moran and Michael Lennington. This book was a game-changer for me—for many of us! They encouraged us to plan in 12-week increments for better productivity.

Be sloppy, just do it! Don't be perfectionistic. Don't be afraid to try!

Add to your Dream List, everything you want to accomplish in the next 90 days. Don't overanalyze it—you'll break it down later! List the big and small things. Do you want to drink more water? Be still and quiet? Grow your email list? Read a book or learn a new skill? Reorganize your bookshelves? Remember family and friends' birthdays with a greeting? Memorize Scripture? Take a shower ("Calgon, take me away")! LIST IT! This list will be essential in helping you plan out your next 12 weeks. The idea is not to get all these things done right now, but to get them on paper.

Do it your way! There is no wrong way!

Suggestion: B.E.L.I.E.F.S. Template

Use the acrostic B.E.L.I.E.F.S. and list everything you want to accomplish under the following dimensions of wellness: Body, Emotions, Livelihood, Intellect, Environment, Family/Friends, Spiritual. Break down the Livelihood dimension further into the various divisions of your company to help you remember to address crucial needs in all areas of your business/ministry.

Honestly, you're probably going to need another piece of paper or a poster board, but here goes!

B.E.L.I.E.F.S.

–**BODY** or Physical Wellness _____

_____

–**Emotional** Wellness _____

_____

–**LIVELIHOOD** or Occupational Wellness _____

_____

_____

_____

- _____
- _____
- _____
- _____
- _____
- _____
- _____

–**Intellectual** Wellness _____

_____

–**Environmental** Wellness _____

_____

–**FAMILY/FRIENDS** or Social Wellness _____

_____

–**Spiritual** Wellness_____

_____

Where do you need to expand your list the most?

_____

Step 8 as you PLAN PURPOSEFULLY is MAKE A LIST and CHECK IT TWICE!

Footnote:
For more information about our use of the B.E.L.I.E.F.S Assessment, check out the Kindle and Print Version Book on Amazon, WELLNESS: The Awareness of the Whole Individual https://t.ly/1nOWB or https://www.amazon.com/Karen-Lindwall-Bourg for an in-depth view of wholeness from a Biblical and balanced perspective.

REVIEW:
https://t.ly/1nOWB

Are you tired of that incomplete and unbalanced feeling? Are you seeking a full and comprehensive life for yourself and those that you serve? Wellness may seem like the buzzword of this century, but wholeness and completeness are necessary for satisfying relationships and entrepreneurial success!

The Word of God tells us that you are complex creatures with a body, soul, and spirit, and it emphasizes that Christ came that you might have life and have it abundantly. To care for ourselves and minister to others without attending to all dimensions of wellness can be neglectful and even dangerous.

Karen Lindwall-Bourg, Grace Edoho-ukwa, and the Associates of RHEMA Counseling bring you *Wellness: The Awareness of the Whole Individual*, providing you effective tools and assessments useful for your own growth and that of your clients, and encouraging living in abundant wellness within the following BELIEFS dimensions:

• Body
• Emotions
• Livelihood
• Intellect
• Environment
• Family/Friends
• Spiritual

Consider the danger in helping a depressed friend or client by discussing their emotions and spiritual conditions without evaluating their medical, environmental, and relationship needs as well. Wellness: The Awareness of the Whole Individual helps you bridge that gap holistically and biblically.

Read this BLOG. Please leave a comment for us to tell us what you've learned.
https://nacwe.org/2017/03/22/7-steps-getting-creatively-unstuck/

Leave a Review, let me know that you left a review, send me your email or snail mail address, and I'll send you the companion WELLNESS Assessment booklet for FREE once you've left a review.

9

ELIMINATE THE "UNNECESSARIES"

My CONFESSIONS:

I'm a "more is more" gal.
I'm a "fear of missing out" girl.
My "wants" automatically become my "needs!"
If I desire it, I am almost positive it IS what God wants for me!

What are Yours?

- _____

- _____

- _____

If you're like me, it's a challenge to eliminate items from this huge list that really don't need to be there, that God never called you to do. But that is the next and most blessed challenge— or let's call it a blessed *opportunity!*

So, go ahead, eliminate items from your list!

SET BOUNDARIES!
PURGE!
WEED!
PRUNE!

Get rid of anything on your list that you need to quit, or that will hinder you from reaching the goal set before you.

Is this sometimes a difficult process? Yes, AND the Lord will help you!

Lisa Turkherst in her book, *The Best Yes*, says, "Every time you say yes to something, you're saying no to something else."

Let me add a *Karen Quip*,

"Every time you say no to something, you are saying YES to something else!"
Karen Lindwall-Bourg
a stronger yes.

My Pruning Story (one of the many...):

My young (first) husband Tim Lindwall, suffered three different types of cancer over a period of four years. He was a wonderful man and I am blessed to have had him in my life for 13 years. When he died, in my moments of grief, I started all sorts of home projects—things that needed to be done AND anything that would numb the pain. My mother worried about me, and not understanding that some of these projects were very therapeutic, she kept calling men from our church to ask them to intervene and help. Here they would come with tools in hand to take over and "relieve" me of these burdensome tasks.

While painting the outside of our house, one of them decided the trees needed to be pruned; and he was right. When they finished the first tree and started on the second, I appeared and was devastated! That first tree looked ruined to me! I refused to let them continue. And as you can imagine that first tree, to this day, 20+ years later – is the healthiest tree in the yard, and the others have suffered along the way (especially the half pruned one)!

Jesus said, *"Every branch in me that does not bear fruit he takes away, and every branch that does bear fruit he **prunes**, that it may bear more fruit."* John 15:2

Pruning is Imperative!

Take the plunge, and boldly remove items from your list that didn't belong and may need to be attended to later.

What are three items that absolutely MUST stay on your list?

- _____
- _____
- _____

What are three items that absolutely MUST be eliminated from your list?

- _____

- _____

- _____

Step 9 as you PLAN PURPOSEFULLY is to ELIMINATE THE UNNECESSARIES.

Read this BLOG. Please leave a comment for us to tell us what you've learned. https://nacwe.org/2011/07/07/twenty-things-to-say-no-to/

Lisa Turkherst in her book, The Best Yes, says, "Every time you say yes to something, you're saying no to something else."

Let me add a *Karen Quip*,

"Every time you say no to something, you are saying YES to something else!"
– Karen Lindwall-Bourg

10

BRACKET SIMILAR ITEMS ON YOUR LIST TOGETHER

I was instructed to use **Bracketing** or **phenomenological reduction** in my Family Therapy Ph.D. Dissertation research. It is a term in the philosophical movement of **phenomenology** describing an act of suspending judgment about the natural world to instead focus on analysis of experience. I was asked not to make any prior judgments or come to any conclusions—and it was hard to do—until I had gathered all the evidence, and to let the research participants teach me what their experiences meant to them.

What am I saying?

Let this Dream List evolve without too much effort from you. I'm reminded of the Beatles' song, "Let it Be!"

Don't Overthink this Process

Suspend prior judgments and guesses as you move forward with this next step. **Don't overthink the process!**

Look at your Dream List from different angles

In this step you will BRACKET similar items on your Dream List together. Sort them. Group them. Watch for patterns as you work.

Think of the process this way. Bracketing is a term also commonly used in photography and is a general technique of taking several shots of the same subject using different camera settings.

Look at your plan from different angles
Bracket/Sort

Synonyms of bracket include group, classify, class, categorize, grade, list, sort, set, place, assign...
To BRACKET also means to enclose words or figures in brackets or place one or more people or things in the same category or group. So, look at this list

from different angles, settings, and perspectives. See what categories and groups you come up with. Group tasks together. For example, you might decide to write a month's worth of blog posts or social media posts in a big batch. This technique works very well with time blocking. It allows you to focus on a huge chunk of work you must do. The idea is to get ahead of your tasks by a significant amount.

Grouping tasks requires some planning. It is good to have an editorial calendar or plan before you when you set up a time to group tasks together. Without editorial planning, this time could easily be wasted by an incessant amount of figuring it out (this is SO me). The goal is to get organized with your tasks and processes and to get work done efficiently.

Look at your list and group similar things together. You will begin to see *patterns* emerge.

You can choose to group things according to interest. Put all the goals or tasks related to entrepreneurship together. Put the items related to physical, emotional, intellectual, environmental, social, and spiritual dimensions together. Put everything related to personal/self-care efforts together. And PLEASE, don't forget YOU.

Chances are the patterns you recognize will develop within the dimensions most important to you. These will be what you need to focus on planning for the next 12 weeks. Remember, you are not trying to get everything on the list done in the next three months. We are being purposeful and strategic in our planning to accomplish some of them. Or, actually, one of them.

Allow yourself to discover new nuances in your big list, and see what you come up with.

Step 10 as you PLAN PURPOSEFULLY is to **BRACKET** SIMILAR ITEMS TOGETHER. Please don't skip this crucial step!

What was your most impactful discovery as you sorted through your list? What are 3–5 TOP categories that emerged as you grouped items together?

- _____
- _____
- _____
- _____
- _____

Read this BLOG. Please leave a comment for us to tell us what you've learned. https://nacwe.org/2014/07/30/focus-on-your-journey/

11

PUT FIRST THINGS FIRST – PRIORITIZE

Pray and ask for wisdom.

Tasha Glover, one of the Kingdom Driven Entrepreneur – Igniter Mentors, says, "Invite God in to every process and task before you begin!"

PRIORITIZE!

I want my priorities to **align with God's priorities**. What would He put first?

First and Foremost, I know I need to **put Him first** in all things.

"But seek first the kingdom of God and His righteousness, and all these things will be added to you." Matthew 6:33

I'm a list gal. I have lists of things to do for my lists of things to do! I know my Dream list is too incredibly long to complete, much less to complete **well**. And I cringe at the thought of spinning my wheels or running in circles.

So Now it is Time to Prioritize.

Choose the most essential course of action, and then...

F.O.C.U.S. – Follow One Course Until Successful

Shelley Hitz of the Christian Book Academy introduced me to the book, *ESSENTIALISM: The Disciplined Pursuit of Less* by Greg McKeown. When you are stretched too thin, overwhelmed, overworked, busy and not as productive as you desire to be, he suggests getting only the *right* things done.

We must discern and select what takes priority and is absolutely essential, eliminate what does not take priority, and focus in on and take action toward making the highest possible concentrated contribution to the tasks on the top of our list.

Reclaim control over your time and your priorities in your life, relationships, and work/ministry.

*"If instead of working on a dozen tasks in a mediocre manner,
you F.O.C.U.S. – Follow One Course Until Successful –
and complete that course with excellence,
you can have an influence and impact on your world
that is infinitely greater than you can imagine!"*

– Karen Lindwall-Bourg

Remember, you are not planning a year here. So, go ahead and place things that will need to develop months down the road into another category. Plan for the next 12 weeks. Look at your list and choose top priorities.

You can move priorities on and off your list later. For example, you may want to hire a babysitter or housekeeper for a few hours a week so you can focus on work. That is definitely a top priority as it gives you more time to write emails and/or talk to clients. Once that goal is accomplished, you can move it off your list and add another priority to your 12-week plan.

Write down your goals.

Most people don't set goals. Very few people write down their goals, and even fewer people have written goals that they *review on a regular basis.* The people who write and review their goals are the high achievers in our society and culture. NACWE Team Member Courtenay Collins shared that she journals every morning and one of the top items on her writing journey before the Lord each day is a hand-written list of her top 10 goals for the year. By September this year, she had accomplished many of her goals. I accept that challenge!

*"You can achieve infinitely more
if you simply write down your goals
and review them on a regular basis."*

– Karen Lindwall-Bourg

What are the top 7 GOALS/PRIORITIES on your list?

What is NUMBER ONE?

Pick things you know you can accomplish. This builds confidence. It also keeps you from getting bogged down in those A.N.Ts—those Automatic Negative Thoughts—and setting yourself up for failure.

Choose at least one goal that will stretch you outside your comfort zone. If you have trouble narrowing it down, please take the time to re-evaluate your list and priorities before continuing. (I admit, I have the most difficulty with this one).

1. _____ ***

2. _____ **

3. _____ *

4. _____

5. _____

6. _____

7. _____

Don't worry, we'll add action steps/tasks to perform each goal listed above soon!

Step 11 as you PLAN PURPOSEFULLY is to Put First Things First – PRIORITIZE

Read this BLOG. Please leave a comment for us to tell us what you've learned. https://nacwe.org/2018/01/23/alexs-tips-for-organizing-your-week-lets-organize/

12

EXAMINE AND ALIGN

Your PURPOSEFUL PLANNING Goals

With Your Character and Core Values, Mission/Tag Line, and Vision Statements

You may have already established these crucial and foundational elements of your business/ministry. If so, I hope you took some time to revisit and refine your core character and values, your mission statement and tagline, and your vision for the next year—especially for this next quarter as you plan your 12-week goals.

What did you add or change? _____

_____

_____

_____

_____

_____

_____

If you are just now taking important steps to define these elements of your business/ministry, I hope you set aside enough time to seek the Lord for direction and complete the process.

If not, continue to refine these elements here, for they will significantly influence your next steps and the course of your endeavors in the future.

What's NEW? _____

_____

_____

_____

_____

_____

_____

_____

Align Your List

When you consider your core values and your mission and vision statements, it is easier to take on your (by now) expertly bracketed list. You have already grouped similar things on your list and discovered emerging patterns. Look at the list again and consider what items take priority AND **align** with your core values, mission, and vision statements.

Now, in your future, when faced with a pivotal decision, you can always refer to these elements and ask whether a new idea or opportunity aligns with your God-given purposes. If no, discard it. If yes, consider it further.

Step 12 as you PLAN PURPOSEFULLY is to EXAMINE and ALIGN your PURPOSEFUL PLANNING Goals with Your Character and Core Values, Mission Statement/Tag Line, and Vision Statements.

PART I
Prepare to Plan
Resources

Pray with Us!
Join our Thursday Prayer Call

Matthew 26
[40] *Then Jesus returned to the disciples and found them sleeping. "Were you not able to keep watch with Me for one hour?" He asked Peter.* [41] *"Watch and pray so that you will not enter into temptation. For the spirit is willing, but the body is weak." ...*

By Phone via Free Conference Calling
All Thursday 8am CST Prayer Calls can be accessed by dialing 1-712-775-8968 / conference code 620259

Check out our NACWE Calendar at http://nacwe.org/calendar and our FREE Group on Facebook at http://facebook.com/groups/NACWEFreedom where we provide community, networking, education and missions' opportunities for you and we talk about planning often.

http://karenbourg.com/calendar

My Prayer For You

Father God,

You Speak to Us and You Hear Us.
Give us ears today to hear from You. Let us hear and see what You have planned for us. Most of all, let Your will be done and Your Kingdom come in our lives, our businesses, and our dreams.

You are Our Provider.
Thank You for assuring us that You have provided all we need – all character, all time, all tools to do what You have called us to do. May we plan well and hear You say, "Well done, good and faithful servant."

You are The Father of Lights.
You tell us, *"Every good gift and every perfect gift is from above, coming down from the Father of lights, with whom there is no variation or shadow due to change."* (James 1:17)

Thank You for every good and perfect gift this past season and, in advance, thank You for every gift in our future!

You Give us Purpose.
We know that our primary purpose is to bring Honor and Glory to You in all that we do. In Colossians 3, You tell us, *"23 Whatever you do, work heartily, as for the Lord and not for men, knowing that from the Lord you will receive the inheritance as your reward. You are serving the Lord Christ."* Give us clarity in our "WHY" and our God-given calling so that we cannot NOT do what You have called us to!

You Impart to Us Character and Value.
Help us choose to be workers of character and to adopt core values that testify to Your Love and Glory. Open our ears to hear the best character and core values for us, our customers, and our business/ministry. Thank you for Your faithfulness. Help us to be faithful.

You have Given Us a Grand Purpose...
– to bring You Glory and Honor in all we do (1 Timothy 1:17). You have called us to work as unto You (Colossians 3:23-24). Help us to define our Mission Statement so that it aligns with Your purposes and callings for us.

You Define Our Vision.
Lord, show us Your Vision(s) for the work You've called us to. Grant us inspiration and insight that can only come from You. Fill our hearts with Your Dreams and Your Desires so we serve others as unto You and in ways that bring You Glory and Honor.

You are a God of ABUNDANCE.
Thank You that You are *able to do **far more abundantly than all we ask or think**, according to Your **power at work within us**...* Give us mustard-seed sized faith to move mountains as You lead us in our businesses/ministries.

You Give Us the Desires of Our Hearts.
Give us the freedom we need to let this pent-up list of dreams and thoughts out onto paper or poster board. Guide the desires of our hearts so they align with Your Heart. May this be a voyage of discovery that helps us plan toward serving You more purposefully this next 12 weeks. Grant us focus, clarity and abundance.

You Provide Clarity and Focus.
We don't want to focus on anything that You did not call us to do. We want to know with certainty that You have called us to a task and then we want to do it wholeheartedly! Give us guidance and clarity as we eliminate things from our list that won't bring You Glory and Honor at this time in the process—that don't need to be before us now.

You are a God of ORDER.
Please Order our steps; help us to see ORDER and patterns in this process; help us to see YOUR ORDER through it all! Then help us as we build on this process step-by-step to identify specific and focused action steps we need to take to PLAN well and in ways that please You.

You have Hope-Filled Plans for Us.
Help us to seek You first, and order our steps, dear Lord, as we prioritize the goals on our lists. We know the plans and purposes You have for us are good and filled with hope according to Your Words in Jeremiah 29:11-14a. We invite You in to every process and task before us. Grant us Your Guidance and Your Path and may all we do bring You Glory and Honor. Choose for us where to start and how to continue so that all we do pleases You.

You are Our Father of Vision and Purpose.
Help us seek You for the right character, values, mission, and vision until we are sure we have heard from You! Grant insights and inspiration so we can always turn to these precepts for direction! May all we do align with Your Kingdom and Your calling on our lives.

In Jesus' Holy Name we pray, Amen.

Blessings,
Karen

PART II

PLAN PURPOSEFULLY

13

1,2,3 – PICK 1 GOAL 2 PLAN FOR 3 MONTHS

Choose 1 goal
2 plan
for
3 months!

Karen Lindwall-Bourg

Pick ONE

I know; if you are like me, you have many goals and it's hard to pick one. How do you pick just ONE? It helps me let go of some and focus on ONE when I remember that I will have several tasks or steps to complete under each major goal. And I can come back to other goals later.

"The approach to excellently mastering a plan is to
choose ONE goal,
outline crucial actionable steps/tasks to complete that goal,
and
be consistent until completion.
Easier said than done—
And it is possible!"

– Karen Lindwall-Bourg

Plan 1

You are more likely to reach your goal

- When you write a specific plan for who, what, when, where, how and why you will work toward this goal
- When you focus on one goal
- When you make your daily actions consistent and repetitive until they become an established habit (it takes 21–31 days to establish a routine; nearer to 60+ days to establish an automatic habit.)

"The way to master more things in the long run is to simply focus on one thing right now." – Karen Lindwall-Bourg

Be Consistent

One of the things we love in our Mastermind Group is the process outlined by C. J. Hayden in her best-selling Book, *Get Clients Now! (™): A 28-Day Marketing Program for Professionals, Consultants, and Coaches.* It works because she expertly helps you create a plan of action tailored especially to you and your potential clients AND she shows you how to outline each step toward your goal on a trackable worksheet. Our Mastermind group helps hold each other accountable and encourages each other along the way; and the process is tried and true—as long as you work the plan.

1 GOAL

At the risk of repeating myself:

"If instead of working on a dozen tasks in a mediocre manner,
you F.O.C.U.S. - Follow One Course Until Successful
and complete that course with excellence –
you can have an influence and impact on your world
that is infinitely greater than you can imagine!"

– Karen Lindwall-Bourg

Step 13 as you PLAN PURPOSEFULLY is to PICK 1 GOAL 2 PLAN for 3 Months

Read this BLOG. Please leave a comment for us and return here to tell us what you've learned.

https://nacwe.org/2013/01/31/the-un-glamorous-ridiculously-obvious-secret-to-achieving-any-goal/

Choose
1 goal
2 plan
for
3 months!

– Karen Lindwall-Bourg

"The way to master more things in the long run is to
simply focus on one thing right now."

– Karen Lindwall-Bourg

14

PLOT YOUR BEST COURSE

Now that you have set your priorities and established your ONE Goal, it is time to plot your course.

Whenever you take a road trip, you don't just get in your car and start driving in any haphazard direction. You plan your trip (destination, budget, dates, method of transportation, food, and lodging), plug the next address into your GPS, and you carefully and strategically plot your course. And, if you're like me, you pray there aren't too many "re-routings."

You then break your trip down into achievable chunks. How far can you ride until you need a break? When and where will you need to stop for gas or food?

In the same way, you plan and plot and "subplot" to achieve your goals in business/ministry.

Look at your top three priorities. Each priority encompasses a major goal for the next 12 weeks.

Next, make a list of all the tasks and steps you need to take under your primary goal to succeed.

According to Franklin Covey in *The 4 Disciplines of Execution*, include lag and lead measures as part of your to-dos and tasks.

For example, let's say you want to have *three more clients* by the end of 12 weeks. The three clients are your ***lag measure***.

Then, there are tasks you can do every day to accomplish this *lag measure*. These **lead measures** are things that you need to do **every day** to accomplish a bigger goal. They **lead** you to your goal.

Your lead measures to recruit three more clients (*lag measure*) in 12 weeks might be

- Adhere to a 24-hour response to all inquiries regarding your services.
- Follow-up with 3 previous inquiries each day.
- Reach out to 10 potential clients each day.

- What else can you think of?

- _____

- _____

- _____

These lead measures turn into what we call **best practices**. We will talk more about practices in the next few segments of this program.

MY EXAMPLE:

PRIMARY LAG Measure GOAL: Increase interactions and membership in NACWE through Reaching Out and Getting to Know Your Campaigns

What is your PRIMARY GOAL?

_____

_____

_____

My Lag Measure: Increase activity, interactions/engagement (Likes/Loves/Wows, Comments, Click throughs, Participation; Pomodoros, Webinars, Prayer Calls, Specials) according to Social Media Analytics

What is your *Lag Measure*?

_____

_____

_____

_____

My *Lead Measures:*

- Interact/Engage myself (and my team members) on Social Media every day.
- Encourage Participants.
- Celebrate Birthdays/Anniversaries/Work-anniversaries.
- Reach out through Private Message (PM), email, text, phone call to each NACWE Elite Member monthly.

- Reach out through PM, email, text, phone call to each NACWE Freedom Member quarterly.

What are your *Lead Measures*?

_____

_____

_____

_____

_____

_____

Best Practices:

- Put Buffer Blocks of Social Media TIME on my calendar each workday...
- Put Strategic Reach Out & Touch Blocks of TIME on my Calendar each week
- More to follow...
- What might be one of your best practices?

_____

...more later

Step 14 as you PLAN PURPOSEFULLY is to PLOT Your Best COURSE

Tell us about your Primary Goal, define your lag measure and your lead measures and then we'll work on best practices to put this awesome plan into action. Keep these steps together to visualize the plan all together as we develop each step or use the Worksheets.

Read this BLOG. Please a comment for us and return here to tell us what you've learned.
https://nacwe.org/2012/01/02/ask-diane-is-a-goal-and-a-dream-the-same-thing/
https://karenbourg.com/2019/10/05/navigating-the-back-roads-of-life/

15

ESTABLISH AND BUILD UPON BEST PRACTICES

Synonyms for best practices include habits, customs, traditions, ways, systems, routines, procedures, rituals, manners, praxes, methods.

Tasks and To-Dos

Your practices – require a lot of practice. They are the to-dos and tasks that you perform on a regular basis. They are the tasks that help you achieve your goals in the long term. Without these ongoing practices, you will not make your dreams come true.

You may develop some practices to stay organized and keep you on task with your lag measures. For example,

- cleaning out your email inbox once a week instead of being distracted by it daily,
- balancing your business accounts at the end of each month, and
- showing up on social media for a video on a consistent basis.

What can you think of?

- _____
- _____
- _____
- _____
- _____

When you break down your priorities into smaller tasks and to-do's, you'll notice that you will develop habits that are recurring practices, systems, and routines.

The Lord is clear in Ephesians 4 and Colossians 3 that we are to put off certain things. He makes that challenging step easier when He tells us what to put on. Revisit your "eliminate/put off" list from earlier steps in this workbook/process.

PUT OFF

What do you need to eliminate further after revisiting your "eliminate/put off" list from earlier steps in this workbook/process?

Before you delve too deeply, PUT OFF some practices you know are hindering your progress.

List a few of these here:

_____

_____

_____

_____

_____

PUT ON

Can you think of new practices you need to adopt and/or old ones you need to resurrect?

_____

_____

_____

_____

_____

_____

Step 15 as you PLAN PURPOSEFULLY is to Establish and Build Upon on BEST Practices.

What is your PRIMARY GOAL?

_____

_____

_____

Lag Measure:

What is your Lag Measure?

_____

_____

_____

_____

Lead Measures:

What are your Lead Measures?

_____

_____

_____

_____

Best Practices:

- What have you established as 3–5 of your best practices (so far)?

- _____

- _____

- _____

- _____

- _____

Before you begin to feel too overwhelmed, I must admit that putting this all together on my own has been, and still is, a challenge. The times I've been most successful have been when I've worked through planning and practices in a small group of like-minded Christian Entrepreneurs.

This is what we do as a small Mastermind Group for maximum efficiency and to achieve extraordinary levels of success worth celebrating @ http://nacwe.org/join.

Read this BLOG. Please leave a comment for us to tell us what you've learned. https://nacwe.org/2014/09/03/brain-power-three-steps-to-control-your-brain-and-envision-success/

16

TIME BLOCKING: STRATEGIC, BUFFER, & BREAK-OUT OR INTENTIONAL, MISCELLANEOUS, & ESCAPE BLOCKS

There is no doubt it can be overwhelming to look at your to-do list, even when you've narrowed the scope to a more manageable 12-week plan. Managing your time can be challenging for anyone.

I know—you're excited!

We're getting ready to break down your God-given BIG and Abundant Goal into daily, weekly, monthly, and quarterly actionable steps!

THINGS ARE GETTING READY TO REALLY HAPPEN!

But before we go there, let me walk you through a practice that has been a game-changer for me and many of our NACWE Sisters.

Time BLOCKing

Time blocking is an easy solution to manage multiple responsibilities and organize your time. It is easy to determine when you have open spaces to concentrate on business, home, and family. It is best to block off these chunks of time on your calendar AND stick to them as much as possible so you can make the best use of your time and focus on one goal at a time.

Consider how long it takes you to perform a task. For example, it may take one to two hours to write a blog, 30 minutes to edit it, and an hour to post it. When you use time blocking, you set aside **two to three and a half hours** during which you focus on blog posting alone. The next few hours might be a block of time for housework. Then maybe the kids come home from school and you plan dinner and homework hours together. You can round out your workday with a half-hour devoted to posting and responding to social media.

Buffer, Breakout and Strategic Time BLOCKS
or
Miscellaneous, Escape, and Intentional Time BLOCKS

As a group, we read the book *The 12-Week Year: Get More Done in 12 Weeks than Others Do in 12 Months*, by Brian Moran & Michael Lennington at the beginning of the year. It was a game changer!

It changed my mindset about setting and accomplishing my goals.

Moran encourages you to plan for 12 weeks instead of 12 months and to focus on those 12 weeks first to reach your primary goal.

He suggests **blocking** off portions of time during your week like this:

- *I call them Miscellaneous Blocks – He calls them Buffer Blocks.* These are times best scheduled for about 30 minutes at a time throughout the week. They are set aside to take care of time-consuming tasks that will help you really buckle down and get the bulk of your work done during the week such as

  - **cleaning off your desk,**
  - **catching up on answering emails,**
  - **setting appointments,**
  - **making quick phone calls,**
  - **even journaling first thing in the morning.**

What would you add to your **Buffer/Miscellaneous Blocks** of time?

_____

_____

_____

_____

_____

- *I call them Escape Blocks – He calls them Breakout Blocks.* These times are usually about three or four hours. Moran suggests scheduling one of these blocks of time every week right in the middle of your work week. That's a big deal for me, but I've rearranged my schedule, so I essentially have the option of a half-day off every Wednesday AND Friday and I am getting more done than ever before. **Breakout/Escape Blocks** may include anything that breaks up a structured and scheduled work week and gives you a re-charge, such as

- **take a nap,** (Oh how I wish!)
- **go for a walk,**
- **photograph the fall leaves,**
- **go to a movie,**
- **meet a friend for lunch.**

What would you add to your **Breakout/Escape Blocks** of time?

_____

_____

_____

_____

_____

- *I call them Intentional Blocks – He calls them Strategic Blocks.* These times—my favorites—are two or three hour blocks of time (as often as you wish) set aside strategically throughout your work week during which you get rid of all distractions and focus on one strategic task at a time that will truly grow your business and ministry efforts/endeavors. **Strategic/Intentional Blocks** of time might include

- **writing a newsletter, sales page, book**
- **creating a course**
- **updating your website and/or social media forums**
- **holding a webinar, seminar**
- **recording a podcast**

What would you add to your Strategic/Intentional Blocks of time?

_____

_____

_____

_____

_____

Time is Tricky!

"For everything there is a season, and a time for every matter under heaven: a time to be born, and a time to die; a time to plant, and a time to pluck up what is planted; a time to kill, and a time to heal; a time to break down, and a time to build up; a time to weep, and a time to laugh; a time to mourn, and a time to dance; a time to cast away stones, and a time to gather stones together; a time to embrace, and a time to refrain from embracing; ..." Ecclesiastes 3:1–8

"But seek first the kingdom of God and his righteousness, and all these things will be added to you." Matthew 6:33

Keep these blocks of time in mind as you plan your BEST Practices and define Daily, Weekly, Monthly & Quarterly actions you will take to make your BIG Dreams come true and to accomplish your most Important GOALS.

Step 16 as you PLAN PURPOSEFULLY is to consider Time BLOCKing.

Read this BLOG. Please leave a comment for us to tell us what you've learned. https://nacwe.org/2015/01/08/overcoming-entrepreneurial-overwhelm/ https://nacwe.org/2014/09/12/7-sanity-savers-organizing-life-work-home-entrepreneur/

17

TRY THE POMODORO TECHNIQUE: OUR FAVORITE TOOL

The Pomodoro Technique is a tool you can use to reach your own objectives; to really **make-it-happen**.

Francesco Cirillo, the owner of Cirillo Consulting in Berlin, created the Pomodoro Technique as a time-management tool to improve productivity and efficiency—to find ways to achieve better results with less time and less effort.

Millions of people have used the Pomodoro Technique to transform their lives, making them more productive and more focused. It teaches you to work within time, instead of struggling against it. It is deceptively simple to learn and life-changing to use.

I've heard several times that Pomodoro is the Italian word for "tomato," and he used a tomato-shaped timer, thus the name.

What is your timer like? Mine is on my laptop.
I'll share it with you: http://online-timers.com/pomodoro-timers

The process helps you manage time toward productivity and efficiency and:

- FOR YOU:
  - Improve motivation
  - Eliminate burnout
  - Communicate to your team
  - Manage distractions and handle interruptions
  - Reduce tension and fear
  - Gain confidence
  - Shift gears (a hard one for me when I feel stuck)
  - Attend to self-care

What else do you need? _____

_____

_____

_____

- EHNHANCE the TASK:

  - Balance tasks
  - Lessen mistakes
  - Reduce the length of work sessions
  - Simplify and organize tasks
  - Improve content
  - Reduce complexity
  - Meet deadlines

What else do you need? _____

_____

_____

_____

_____

Before you Begin:

- **Gather all materials** needed
- **Commit** to spending 25 uninterrupted minutes on the **(1)** task you've chosen (*It's just 25 minutes.*);
- **Block off a 2–2 ½ hour period of time** to work;
- **Choose the (1) task** you'd like to work on – something that deserves your full, undivided attention;
- **Define your objectives;**
- **Predict how much time/effort** this task requires;
- **Plan** how you will handle inevitable interruptions; and
- Stick to your plan.
- **Focus on Efficiency.**

- **Other:** _____

_____ _____

_____ _____

_____ _____

_____ _____

During your Pomodoro Session:

- **Set your timer** for 25/5/25/5/25/5/25 minutes – we use this online timer very successfully http://online-timers.com/pomodoro-timers
- **Work diligently** on the (1) task. 2 Timothy 2:15 ESV says, *"Do your best to present yourself to God as one approved, a worker who has no need to be ashamed, rightly handling the word of truth."*
- **Manage distractions.** If you suddenly realize you have something else you need to do, write it down on a sheet of paper for later, so it won't keep you distracted now.
- **Track your progress.**
- DO **take 5-minute breaks**—breathe, meditate, grab a cup of coffee, go for a short walk, or do something else relaxing—i.e., not work-related.
- **Take a LONGER break** after every 4 Pomodoro (25-minute) sessions. (Your brain will use this time to assimilate new information and rest before the next work session.)
- **Do it again!**

- **Other:** _____

_____

_____

_____

_____

My POMODORO Checklist

Checkbox		Example:
	Materials Gathered	*Laptop, Timer, extra paper*
	Commitment Made	
	Calendar Blocked Off	
	Task Chosen	*Complete 1 BLOG*
	Objectives Defined	• *Outline* • *Compose* • *Post*
	Prediction	*2.5 hours* *9:00 Outline/break* *9:30 Write/break* *10:00 Write/break* *10:30 Edit/Create Canva Graphics* *11:00 Post in Wordpress and to Social Media sites*
	Plan against interruptions	*Phone in other room, Scrap paper to dump distractions on*
	Other: _____	
	Set Timer	
	Work Diligently	
	Track Progress	
	Take Breaks	
	Other: _____	

Step 17 as you PLAN PURPOSEFULLY is to Try the Pomodoro Technique.

This is another reason to join up with the NACWE group work sessions Monday through Thursday. NACWE Sisters can help!

A game changer for me and our NACWE Team has been the practice of blocking off those strategic portions of time and attending our NACWE "Happening Pomodoro" Sessions on weekday mornings. We've made progress incomparable to previous years!

You should **join us** because everyone who shows up is really cranking out the work and making things happen.

NACWE Pomodoro Work Sessions:
Monday, Tuesday, Wednesday &/or Thursdays (you choose)
9:00–11:30 AM CST
https://goo.gl/r32zu3

Read this BLOG. Please leave a comment for us to tell us what you've learned.
https://nacwe.org/2013/03/21/procrastination-three-tips-to-help-you-move-past-it/

18

BEST PRACTICES

18a

DO-ABLE DAILY PRACTICES

One of the daily practices that works best for me is setting up a 25-minute *Buffer* Block of Time to get small tasks out of the way before I buckle down to a larger, more demanding task.

Then, I enjoy showing up for the NACWE Pomodoro sessions for **Strategic** Blocks of time. We show up in a Zoom.com room each morning.

Here's our schedule:

15 minutes: We share what we are working on and any prayer requests we have. We pray for one another.

Then, **audio is turned off and video is hidden** to lessen distractions.

25 minutes:	Work Session
5 minutes:	break
25 minutes:	Work Session
5 minutes:	break
25 minutes:	Work Session
5 minutes:	break
25 minutes:	Work Session
= 2 hours of work time	

15 minutes: We debrief, celebrate our wins, encourage one another for the coming day, and PRAY again!

This blocked off time allows me to set aside a very blessed two and a half hours to work on other practices.

Common daily practices during this strategic block of time could include:

- journaling your gratitude to God
- returning phone calls
- setting a limited time to answer emails
- spending specific time on posting to social media
- writing blog posts

What can you think of?

- _____

- _____

- _____

- _____

- _____

Executing daily practices will help you establish a daily routine for getting things done. Setting up regular practices is part of Purposeful Planning. As with all practices and planning, I highly recommend putting these things on your calendar. If you're like me, if it's not on the calendar, it usually doesn't take priority and sometimes doesn't get done at all.

Step 18a as you PLAN PURPOSEFULLY is establishing Do-able DAILY Practices.

What is your PRIMARY GOAL?

_____

_____

_____

Lag Measure:

What is your Lag Measure?

_____

_____

_____

_____

_____

Lead Measures:

What are your Lead Measures?

_____

_____

_____

_____

_____

DAILY Best Practices:

- What are a few of your DAILY best practices?

  _*Miscellaneosus* _____

  _____

  _Intentional _____

  _____

  _____

  _____

  _____

Read this BLOG. Please leave a comment for us and return here to tell us what you've learned.
https://nacwe.org/2011/11/21/a-daily-thankful-attitude/
https://nacwe.org/2012/07/06/27-brands-and-products-i-use-on-a-daily-basis/

18

BEST PRACTICES

18b

WISE WEEKLY PRACTICES

The same routine day after day can become a challenge for varying reasons. You will probably need to set up a day each week to accomplish certain tasks in your 12-week plan that don't require daily attention. On certain days of the week you may

- Worship
- Attend networking meetings or hold your own meetings
- PLAN
- Write
- Take a Course/Study
- Don't forget Pizza Night!

What can you think of?

- _____
- _____
- _____
- _____
- _____

Again, **put these events on your calendar.** Protect the scheduling of these weekly practices. Schedule around them. They are essential to making your dreams come true. They are the foundation of accomplishing all you have purposefully planned.

Step 18b as you PLAN PURPOSEFULLY is to establish Wise Weekly Practices.

LIST DAILY Best Practices:

- What are a few of your DAILY best practices?

_____

_____

_____

_____

_____

_____

_____

List WEEKLY Best Practices:

- What are a few of your WEEKLY best practices? _____

_____

_____

_____

_____

_____

_____

Begin considering Monthly/Quarterly Practices.

Let us help you! This is what we do as a small/Mastermind Group for maximum efficiency and to achieve extraordinary levels of success worth celebrating @ http://nacwe.org/join .

Read this BLOG. Please leave a comment for us and return here to tell us what you've learned.
https://nacwe.org/2018/11/12/be-strong-and-courageous-so-you-will-have-success/

18

BEST PRACTICES

18c

MANAGEABLE MONTHLY PRACTICES

There are some things that can wait. Of course, they need to be done, but not today or even this week. When you organize your tasks into daily, weekly, and monthly categories you can focus on the specific tasks that get you closer to achieving your goals.

Personally, I tend to do another brain dump of all the things I need to do at the beginning of each new month. I will list everything that needs to be done that month—sometimes, even a bit further into the future.

Here is the kicker: **I think I must do it all today.**

Something happens in my brain, and this dire urgency to get everything done as fast as possible overwhelms me—it is a bit self-defeating when we talk about Purposeful Planning. So, the way around this is to really figure out what needs to be done regularly based on the day, week, month, or quarter.

Monthly activities may include

- Meetings & Events: for the NACWE Team, Networking Meetings...
- Planning and outlining the Social Media Posts for the next month or quarter
- Planning and outlining the Newsletters for the next month or quarter
- Planning and outlining the Blogs for the next month or quarter
- Planning and outlining the Quarterly Retreats, VIP Coaching Days, and next year's #2020NACWEConference—more ahead of time than I usually do, I HOPE!

What can you think of?

- _____

- _____

- _____

- _____

- _____

LIST DAILY Best Practices:

- What are a few of your DAILY best practices?

_____

_____

_____

_____

_____

_____

_____

List WEEKLY Best Practices:

- What are a few of your WEEKLY best practices?

_____

_____

_____

_____

_____

_____

List MONTHLY Best Practices:

- What are a few of your MONTHLY best practices?

_____

_____

_____

_____

_____

_____

Begin thinking of those quarterly actions you'll need to attend to.

Now make sure all these items have been filtered through your Purpose, Your **WHY**, your core values, and mission & vision statements; and ensure they align with your God-given calling and primary Goal for the next 90-days.

PUT THEM ON YOUR CALENDAR!

Step 18c as you PLAN PURPOSEFULLY is to plan Manageable Monthly Practices.

Read this BLOG. Please leave a comment for us and return here to tell us what you've learned.
https://karenbourg.com/2020/01/31/be-an-entrepreneur-with-gumption/

18

BEST PRACTICES

18d

QUARTERLY QUEST BEST PRACTICES

When you implement 12-week or 90-day Purposeful Planning strategies, there is a natural rhythm that begins to form and a consistent tendency to reevaluate your goals and steps at the end of three months. It is our goal to PLAN together quarterly. Each new quarter becomes a time to congratulate and reward yourself for all you accomplished in the previous quarter. It is a great time to keep good practices in place and rethink things that didn't work as well as you would have liked them to. It is a time for relief because you don't get stuck in a pattern that isn't working for you.

Reset and Celebrate

Quarterly practices can also include taking a little vacation, a break from the work and routine—even one that works as well as this one! Some of the reset and celebratory goals you can set for each quarter review are:

- *CeLeBrAtE!*
- Record your best practices in some detail so you can keep up the good work.
- Re-Evaluate, Tweak, and/or Eliminate any practices that didn't work well for you.
- Take a desperately needed long weekend or week-long break or vacation.
- Close up loose ends or complete a monthly or weekly task left undone so far.
- Balance the Book$
- Prepare for the next launch, offer, service, program, product, other...
- Recruit and Schedule Presenters for Educational Programs
- Continue working toward the YEARLY Conference
- DREAM!

What can you think of?

- _____

- _____

- _____

- _____

- _____

Keep in mind that some of these tasks may need to be broken down into monthly, weekly, and daily practices.

LIST DAILY Best Practices:

- What are a few of your DAILY best practices?

List WEEKLY Best Practices:

- What are a few of your WEEKLY best practices?

List MONTHLY Best Practices:

- What are a few of your MONTHLY best practices?

_____

_____

_____

_____

_____

_____

List QUARTERLY Best Practices:

- What are a few of your QUARTERLY best practices?

_____

_____

_____

_____

_____

_____

Step 18d as you PLAN PURPOSEFULLY is to implement Quarterly Quest Practices.

This is what we do as a small Mastermind group when we work through C. J. Hayden's Get Clients NOW Program each quarter.

We call our Program the **PDF² Program** – we Plan, Design and Follow Through!

Webpage
http://karenbourg.com/PlanDesignFollowThrough

Facebook Group
By Invitation
https://www.facebook.com/groups/PlanDesignFollowThrough/

or

Join us on one of our Quarterly Writing Retreats
http://karenbourg.com/RetreattoWrite

Read this BLOG. Please leave a comment for us and return here to tell us what you've learned.
https://nacwe.org/2011/12/15/take-a-step-plan-for-success-in-2012/

19

POOH THE PIDDLY PRACTICES

Piddly practices are those things that need to be done that you might consider mundane. They frustrate you. They distract you. However, they cannot be skipped, or things will get out of hand!

At home, these piddly practices can include household tasks that help you keep your peace of mind like loading the dishwasher, keeping up with the laundry, taking out the trash, sorting the mail, sweeping the porches, or meal planning and grocery shopping. Staying on top of piddly practices can be a source of great frustration, but in the end may help stave off overwhelm when you are an entrepreneur.

My list of confessions:

- loading the dishwasher – once I discovered I could load the WHOLE dishwasher in the time it took for my coffee to brew I felt so free!;
- keeping up with the laundry – we (make that I) only do laundry on weekends, and one of our sons helps fold and hang. Yay!;
- taking out the trash – "the new deal" = I take it to one level and dear husband does the rest;
- sorting the mail – instead of letting it pile up, so I see the big stack (which is mostly junk by the way and totally overwhelms me), I sort as it comes in;
- sweeping the porches – when the Grandorables come over we incorporate this task into some of our outdoor time, killing two birds with one stone;
- meal planning and grocery shopping – confession, I can barely do toast, so I haven't figured this one out yet! What's your solution?

What's on your **at home** list? And what creative solutions have you or can you come up with?

- _____ – _____
- _____ – _____
- _____ – _____
- _____ – _____
- _____ – _____

Are not two sparrows sold for a penny? And not one of them will fall to the ground apart from your Father. But even the hairs of your head are all numbered. Fear not, therefore; you are of more value than many sparrows."
Matthew 10:30-31

At work, piddly practices may differ from person to person and business to business. Some of those mundane practices that must be done could include cleaning out that e-Mail inbox, shopping for work, gathering tools for each project, making phone calls, editing ANYTHING, creating graphics, posting MOST THINGS on social media, or remembering celebration days.

My list confessions:

• cleaning out that e-Mail inbox – UGH!;
• shopping for work – I HATE shopping, luckily, there's Amazon;
• gathering tools for each project – setting it all out and cleaning it all up later drives me batty! I've begun setting up different work stations for different tasks in my office – this has helped;
• making phone calls – I'm an introvert—I hate the phone, but if I put this task on my calendar with time limits, once I dive in, I actually enjoy it. (sometimes...);
• editing ANYTHING – I never seem to finish (perfectionism issues) so I edit once, then send it to someone on my team. They are better at it anyway;
• creating graphics – when I try to do it myself, I end up having to get help anyway. I HIRE a creative someone most of the time;
• posting MOST THINGS on social media – thank God for schedulers like Co-Schedule or HootSuite or Facebook Scheduler or Post Planner; or
• remembering celebration days – I really do want to tell you HaPpY BiRtHdAy! Has anyone got this one down to a fine art? I need help!

What's on your **at work** list? And what creative solutions have you or can you come up with?

• _____ – _____
• _____ – _____
• _____ – _____
• _____ – _____

Step 19 as you PLAN PURPOSEFULLY is to Pooh the PIDDLY Practices.

Read this BLOG. Please leave a comment for us to tell us what you've learned. https://nacwe.org/2011/06/22/proven-strategies-to-balancing-your-life/

20

SET BOUNDARIES AND BE PROACTIVE

Set Boundaries

You might wonder what boundaries have to do with Purposeful Planning. If you haven't read the book, *Boundaries: When to Say Yes, How to Say No To Take Control of Your Life* by Henry Cloud and John Townsend, I highly recommend it. Your plan won't work smoothly until you learn what to say "Yes" to and when, "No" to and when, and to realize that those two little words will help you take control of your plan. *This is a daily challenge for me.*

You don't have to say yes to everyone's requests or take responsibility for the plans of others.

You *do* need to focus on your God-given plan within your own limits.

It is possible to set legitimate boundaries in a loving way, manage your relationships and your plan even in this digital age, and to do this without feeling guilty or afraid or selfish. If you don't establish boundaries that you can enforce and others will respect, it will be exceedingly difficult to stick with your plan. Boundaries allow you to stick with your practices and time blocks. Keeping good boundaries allows you to honor the things you put on your schedule. It also gives you the space to honor your own wishes and dreams.

Setting healthy boundaries makes me MORE, not less available for family and friends, and at more appropriate times.
- Karen Lindwall-Bourg

What do you need to do to set healthy and legitimate boundaries?

*   Make a prayerful decision about your *yeses*
*   Make a prayerful decision about your *noes*
*   Commit to stick to your convictions!

What about you?

- _____

- _____

- _____

- _____

- _____

Be Proactive

Prepared Christians are ready to act. Therefore, they are proactive.

Jesus tells us we must be ready for His return. *"You too, be ready; for the Son of Man is coming at an hour that you do not expect"* (Luke 13:40).

Paul tells us to be ready for every good deed. *"Remind them to be subject to rulers, to authorities, to be obedient, to be ready for every good deed"* (Titus 3:1).

And Peter tells us to be ready to give an answer to everyone who asks about our hope. *"...but sanctify Christ as Lord in your hearts, always being ready to make a defense to everyone who asks you to give an account for the hope that is in you. . ."* (1 Peter 3:15).

You must be proactive to be prepared and be ready!

I've spent way too many entrepreneurial hours passively reacting to what happens to me and within my organization; it almost always leads to frustration and miscommunication. You want to be proactive. Setting boundaries and planning purposefully need to be some of the most proactive things you do as an entrepreneur.

Purposeful Planning is a proactive process. It includes putting things on your calendar and not moving them (within reason). Life, in general, often influences your planning to an extent, but proactive planning will help you keep your yes and no commitments for your business sacred.

Passive reacting involves putting out fires; for example, reacting to an email instead of writing the blog post you intended to write.

Proactive planning enables you to honor your plan and wait until later to answer that email. When you plan proactively and purposefully you stay focused on your daily practices, your routine, and your goals.

What does a more proactive plan (vs. passive reacting) look like in your organization?

- My Plan is complete, reviewed, revised and is ON MY CALENDAR.
- Prepare to be Ready to be Proactive.
- Note to Karen: ALLOW FOR PREP TIME.

What about you?

- _____

- _____

- _____

- _____

- _____

Step 20 as you PLAN PURPOSEFULLY is to Set Boundaries and Be Proactive!

Read this BLOG. Please leave a comment for us to tell us what you've learned.
https://nacwe.org/2014/11/01/7-tips-partnering-with-success/

PART II
Plan Purposefully
Resources

Get it done!

Join our M–Th POMODORO Work Sessions at https://goo.gl/r32zu3. Share what you are working on and any prayer requests you have. Work and Break, Work and Break, Rinse & Repeat. Then, Celebrate!

You should join us because everyone who shows up is really cranking out the work and making things happen.

NACWE Pomodoro Work Sessions
Monday, Tuesday, Wednesday &/or Thursdays (you choose)
9:00–11:30 AM CST

Work Together!
This is what we do as a small/Mastermind group when we work through C.J. Hayden's Get Clients NOW Program each quarter.

We call our Program the *PDF² Program* – we **P**lan, **D**esign and **F**ollow Through!

> *"Two hearts are better than one; four hearts are better than two..."*
> *– Karen Lindwall-Bourg*

Webpage
http://karenbourg.com/PlanDesignFollowThrough

Facebook Group
By Invitation
https://www.facebook.com/groups/PlanDesignFollowThrough/

or

**Join us on one of our Quarterly Writing Retreats
http://karenbourg.com/RetreattoWrite**

My Prayer for You

Lord,

<u>You Know the Plans You Have for Us</u>.
Help us to know the plans You have for us so succinctly that we cannot NOT do what You have called us to do. We struggle to focus on only one primary goal at a time and therefore are not always successful to completion. Show us Your Way and give us the Desires of Your Heart—make them our desires. Help us to reach the goals You have laid out before us, one at a time!

<u>You Protect Us and Our Work/Ministry</u>.
We are good at planning and plotting—or so we think. It's getting in the car and getting started on the journey that trips us up. Help us to be sure the plans we have and the plotted course we want to take to reach our goal are from You, ordained by You, desired by You, planted within us by You. Build a hedge of protection around us so we do not go astray and protect us from harm. May every step we take on this path be pleasing to You and draw others on our shared path to You.

<u>Teach us Your Ways</u>
...so, we can walk in them. Best Practices must line up with Your Will and Your Plan for us. Lead us step-by-step toward a plan that brings success and honors You.

<u>You Have Ordained All Time for Us</u>
...perfectly. There ARE enough hours in our day because You ordained a 24-hour day and all we need to do within those 24-hours. Help us to use our time wisely, to block portions of time on our work calendars in ways that enhance our ability to get the work done, and in ways that please YOU! You tell us to *Do your best to present yourself to God as one approved, a worker who has no need to be ashamed, rightly handling the word of truth.* 2 Timothy 2:15 ESV

<u>You Appreciate Efficiency</u>.
We want to be diligent and efficient in doing the work You have called us to do. Help us as we use great tools like the Pomodoro Technique, to be more productive and efficient.

<u>You Care about Every Second</u>.
You count and care for the stars in the sky, the grains of sand in the sea, the hairs on our heads. You created years, quarters, months, weeks, days, hours, minutes, seconds. We want to use them wisely for Your glory and honor. Help us to do just that. So, You care about our year, our quarter, our month, our

week, our day, our hour, our minute, our second. WOW! Help us to plan and work wisely knowing that You care and to be grateful for Your Care.

You Give Us Every Moment We Need to Do What You Have Called Us to DO. Help us to focus only on those monthly tasks that will help us to achieve our goals and serve our clients well. Help us to focus only on those quarterly tasks that will help us to achieve our goals and serve our clients well. Again, You have granted us enough months in a year and in a lifetime to accomplish what You've called us to do. May we be dedicated and diligent to fulfill the calling You have placed on our lives.

For by him all things were created, in heaven and on earth, visible and invisible, whether thrones or dominions or rulers or authorities—all things were created through him and for him. And he is before all things, and in him all things hold together. Colossians 1:16-17 ESV

You Are Concerned About Everything That Happens to Us.
Thank YOU! Because You are concerned about everything that happens to us, we can bring even the smallest concern to You in prayer, knowing that You care about us and watch over us. You love us and care what happens to us. You number every hair on our heads (Matthew 10:30–31) and You sent us Your SON. You are so great that even the very smallest detail of the universe—from the most distant galaxy, to the earth, to the smallest seed, to the sub-atomic particle—ALL are under Your control. You created everything and You hold it all together (Colossians 1:16-17). We thank YOU! Help us to remember this when we feel a task is mundane or frustrating.

You are a God of Acton.
The key word here is "action!" Help us to take the steps needed to plan, to prepare to do the work You've called us to do, and to implement the plan well so we hear You say, "Well done, good and faithful servant!" Help us to *set healthy boundaries that will make us MORE, not less available for family and friends, and at more appropriate times.*

**Blessings,
Karen**

"TWO HEARTS ARE BETTER THAN ONE; FOUR HEARTS ARE BETTER THAN TWO..."

– Karen Lindwall-Bourg

PART III

PROGRESS ALONG THE PLAN PATH

21

PLAN TO TRACK, BE TENACIOUS, STEADFAST, <u>AND</u> YET, FLEXIBLE

Plan to Track Your Progress

Tracking your progress, task by task, is one of the most encouraging and efficient ways to keep up your momentum and reach your goals. Make a list of your daily, weekly, and monthly practices. Check them off as you complete them. Are you, like me, anxious to place that checkmark? When you check off a weekly task, you might want to tick off and give yourself credit for all the days of the week. At the end of your week, month, and quarter, take a peek at all the checked boxes and celebrate your accomplishments.

Be Tenacious

Be Tenacious! Synonyms for tenacious include – stubborn, obstinate, **resolute, firm, persistent,** insistent, dogged, determined, steadfast, inflexible (antonym – irresolute). Which is your favorite? Which words would you want someone to use to describe you at your work?

My favorite is **steadfast!**

"Therefore, my beloved brothers, be steadfast, immovable, always abounding in the work of the Lord, knowing that in the Lord your labor is not in vain."
1 Corinthians 15:58 ESV

Be steadfast! Be immovable! Abound! "…in the Lord your labor is not in vain!"

To complete tasks toward a focused and clear goal, you will have to establish a **stick-to-itiveness** – a **steadfastness** – that carries you through to the end. We have already said this requires working through a Purposeful Planning process in detail (like this one, of course) with a clear goal in mind and strategic steps defined to take you to completion and success.

Be Flexible

Synonyms for flexible include – **supple**, lithe, elastic, plastic, stretchy, **bendable**, springy, malleable, bendy, (antonyms – rigid, stiff), **adaptable**, **accommodating**, variable, compliant, open, acquiescent, tractable, amenable, docile, (antonyms – intractable, rigid). Which is your favorite? Which words would you want someone to use to describe you at your work?

> *"The plans of the heart belong to man,*
> *but the answer of the tongue is from the Lord.*
> *All the ways of a man are pure in his own eyes,*
> *but the Lord weighs the spirit.*
> ***Commit your work to the Lord,***
> ***and your plans will be established."***
> Proverbs 16:1-3

God has given you the desires of your heart (aligned with the desires of His Heart) and the intelligence and emotional will to see your plans through. I don't always trust that enough, do you?

His Will Be Done!

Listen and be flexible!

Be aware that as you work through, He will guide and redirect you.

Then work forward with tenacity, steadfastness, and flexibility. I LOVE those words!

Tracking Tools

Put together a worksheet to guide you along the way. You may want to create it in a Word document and transfer it to an Excel sheet later. I LIVE in Excel and Google Sheets. My coach for many years preferred Word and Google Documents. We were constantly asking each other for permission to convert our worksheets and tools into another format to suit our temperament and work styles.

Do what works for you.

Here is a suggestion:

My Primary GOAL:

_____

_____

_____

Challenges:

_____

_____

_____

_____

_____

Current status:

_____

_____

_____

BIG Dream:

_____

_____

_____

My Reward:

_____

_____

_____

_____

_____

Strategies:

_____

_____

_____

_____

My Statement: I will...

_____

_____

_____

_____

_____

TOP 3-5 tasks to accomplish this goal:

1. _____

2. _____

3. _____

4. _____

5. _____

PURPOSEFUL PLANNING

Daily Actions	Weekly Actions	Monthly Actions	Quarterly Actions

Self Care:

_____

_____

_____

_____

_____

Step 21 as you PLAN PURPOSEFULLY is to PLAN to TRACK, Be Tenacious and Flexible

Read this BLOG. Please leave a comment for us to tell us what you have learned. https://nacwe.org/2013/01/21/the-3-ingredients-in-the-inspired-women-succeed-recipe-for-christianwomen-entrepreneurs/ https://nacwe.org/2014/05/20/if-you-treasure-it-then-measure-it/

22

READY, SET, TAKE ACTION!

"Commit your work to the Lord, and your plans will be established." Proverbs 16:3

FINALLY!

You are going to take action, see progress, and experience results.

There WILL Be Challenges Along the Way

Will there be challenges along the way? There already have been, am I right? And there will be others.

Obstacles are inevitable and we rarely have control over them. How you respond to obstacles is what really makes the ultimate difference in the long run. **Choose.** Realizing this fact of life is empowering, and taking steps to care for yourself and your masterful plan along the way will ensure that you stay encouraged and determined.

Overcoming Obstacles

Think of some things you can do to **remember** your "WHY" and the calling and the process of creating the plan. Remind yourself that you will soon be seeing more light at the end of the tunnel. Do what you need to do to boost your confidence and dive back in again. Be willing to be tenacious and flexible as you march forward. **Post your "WHY" above your workspace.**

Adjust along the way; none of this plan is etched in stone. In our Mastermind group we often share our plan with others for feedback, a reality check per se, encouragements and sometimes advice toward adjustments that need to be made!

What are some adjustments you need to make for now?

- _____

- _____

- _____
- _____
- _____
- _____
- _____

Sometimes, when you don't reach your goal in the time you allotted or in the way you envisioned, it can be **a blessing in disguise**. At least you are reminded to re-focus on your WHY, your passion. Those who focus on the outcome or goal often miss the mark. Your Why is what motivates you to achieve in the first place. So, adapt, improvise, and overcome obstacles along the way.

Thank God for the **blessing in disguise**.

_____

_____

_____

_____

_____

The hardest part is completed. The plan is written (Habakkuk 2:2), it is concise, it is organized step-by-step, and it will lead to success. Focus on your dream, your passion; and pursue it to the fullest. The best is yet to come!

Step 22 as you PLAN PURPOSEFULLY is Ready, Set, TAKE ACTION!

Read this BLOG. Please leave a comment for us to tell us what you have learned! https://nacwe.org/2013/01/16/staying-committed-to-your-business/

23

FIND A MENTOR OR PARTNER OR GROUP

*Truly, I say to you, whatever you bind on earth shall be bound in heaven, and whatever you loose on earth shall be loosed in heaven. Again I say to you, **if two of you agree** on earth about anything they ask, it will be done for them by my Father in heaven. For where two or three are gathered in my name, there am I among them.* Matthew 18:18-20

You are NOT Alone!

There is no doubt this entrepreneur thing cannot be done alone. To really be successful it is important to find a community of like-minded folks who will pray with you and encourage you, perhaps who will walk alongside you all the way. I believe one of the greatest challenges as an entrepreneur is believing you are alone and feeling as if no one else is struggling in the same way you are.

You are not alone!

You Don't Need an Accountability Cohort

In The 12-Week Year, Moran and Lennington's view of accountability changed things for me. They say that we misunderstand the concept of accountability in business and life. We have come to believe that accountability is something that is imposed upon another like consequences.

Therefore, most people want nothing to do with accountability!

Instead, they say, "The very nature of accountability rests in the understanding that each and every one of us has freedom of choice. It is this freedom of choice that is the foundation of accountability." You have choices and when you choose to do something, you are empowered and able to tap into your best resources and determine your actions and results, and consequences. It's up to you and affects everything you do, from your relationships to your business. It's about your choice and taking ownership of your choices – being empowered, surrounded by possibilities, and achieving greatness. They say,

"The only person who can hold you accountable for anything is you, and to be successful you must develop the mental honesty and courage to own your thinking, actions, and results."

Let's be honest and courageous to own our thinking, actions, and results!
I love that!

You and I May Need a Mentor or Partner

⁹ Two are better than one, because they have a good reward for their toil.
¹⁰ For if they fall, one will lift up his fellow. But woe to him who is alone when he falls and has not another to lift him up!
¹¹ Again, if two lie together, they keep warm, but how can one keep warm alone?
¹² And though a man might prevail against one who is alone, two will withstand him
*—**a threefold cord is not quickly broken.***
Ecclesiastes 4 (ESV)

Remember—two heads (I like to say hearts) are better than one; four hearts are better than two, etc.... Like-minded entrepreneurs can help along the journey. A good business/ministry buddy is also great for encouragement, motivation, brainstorming and staying focused. As a Christian entrepreneur, it's also great to have someone to share with in prayer.

And the two or three or four of you get to define what partnering and mentorship looks like and doesn't look like. You know what you need; ask for it! You know what you don't need; communicate those boundaries too!

Step 23 as you PLAN PURPOSEFULLY is to FIND an ACCOUNTABILITY PARTNER

Read this BLOG. Please leave a comment for us to tell us what you have learned. https://nacwe.org/2015/11/01/10-ways-to-be-a-great-mentor/

24

STICK-TO-IT!

Where does that Stick-to-It resolve come from?

The Will to Stick-to-It comes from a Good Challenge.

One of my coaches challenged me well by saying she thought I really didn't like what I was doing. In a Facebook writing group, the leader once said if we weren't writing what we wanted to write, we probably did not really want to write it.

In both cases I was surprised by my strong reaction.

First, I checked my spirit and attitude and reminded myself not to whine so much.

Then I asked the Lord to give me direction.

In both cases I ended up re-committing to the task and sticking-to-it more diligently. I pressed on instead of giving up. In another case, I drastically changed the way I was doing my work and was quickly blessedly pointed in a new direction.

There are going to be challenges and upsets. There are going to be lots of times you may feel like quitting or at least delaying the current process or task before you.

The Will to Stick-to-It is Yours

- Remember your **Purpose**, your **WHY**.

  Go and Bear Fruit – *You did not choose me, but I chose you and appointed you that you should go and bear fruit and that your fruit should abide, so that whatever you ask the Father in my name, he may give it to you.* John 15:16

- Remember how lives (including yours) will be **influenced** if you persist and endure.

  Be a Leader – *You are the salt of the earth, but if salt has lost its taste, how shall its saltiness be restored? It is no longer good for anything except to be thrown out and trampled under people's feet. You are the light of the world. A city set on a hill cannot be hidden. Nor do people light a lamp and put it under a basket, but on a stand, and it gives light to all in the house. In the same way, let your light shine before others, so that they may see your good works and give glory to your Father who is in heaven.* Matthew 5:13-16

- **Commit** to the vision and goal, and carry on.

  Proceed with Hope – *For I know the plans I have for you, declares the Lord, plans for welfare and not for evil, to give you a future and a hope.* Jeremiah 29:11

- **Write it out** and diligently continue.

  Write the Vision – *And the Lord answered me: Write the vision; make it plain on tablets, so he may run who reads it. For still the vision awaits its appointed time; it hastens to the end—it will not lie. If it seems slow, wait for it; it will surely come; it will not delay.* Habakkuk 2:2-3

- Talk to your **partner(s) and mentor(s)**: ask for encouragement, then keep at it!

  Be Encouraged and Encourage Others – *Therefore encourage one another and build one another up, just as you are doing.* 1 Thessalonians 5:11

Step 24 as you PLAN PURPOSEFULLY is to **Stick-to-It!**

Read this BLOG. Please leave a comment for us to tell us what you have learned. https://nacwe.org/2017/03/22/7-steps-getting-creatively-unstuck/

25

THE OPPOSITE OF PROCRASTINATION IS ACTION!

Procrastination is a puzzling and frustrating phenomenon.

It is irrational. It is harmful. It is against our best intentions.

So why do we delay the very things we want to do? Why do we postpone what we know is best for us?

Self-ASSESSMENT:
Are you being sinful?

Wait! This sounds so familiar! Paul talked of this struggle in Romans 7:

> *14-16 I can anticipate the response that is coming: "I know that all God's commands are spiritual, but I'm not. Isn't this also your experience?" Yes. I'm full of myself—after all, I've spent a long time in sin's prison. What I don't understand about myself is that* **I decide one way, but then I act another,** *doing things I absolutely despise. So, if I can't be trusted to figure out what is best for myself and then do it, it becomes obvious that* <u>God's command is necessary</u>.*
> *17-20 But I need something more! For if I know the law but still can't keep it, and if the power of sin within me keeps sabotaging my best intentions, I obviously need help! I realize that I don't have what it takes. I can will it, but I can't do it. I decide to do good, but I don't really do it;* **I decide not to do bad, but then I do it anyway. My decisions, such as they are, don't result in actions.** *Something has gone wrong deep within me and gets the better of me every time.*
> *21-23 It happens so regularly that it's predictable. The moment I decide to do good, sin is there to trip me up. I truly delight in God's commands, but it's pretty obvious that not all of me joins in that delight. Parts of me covertly rebel, and just when I least expect it, they take charge.*
> *24 I've tried everything and nothing helps. I'm at the end of my rope. Is there no one who can do anything for me? Isn't that the real question?*
> *25* <u>*The answer, thank God, is that Jesus Christ can and does. He acted to set things right in this life of contradictions where I want to serve*</u>

God with all my heart and mind, but am pulled by the influence of sin to do something totally different.
The Message

He is obviously saying sin/our sinful nature plays a part in our putting off what we know we should do. Yikes!

In what ways might you be sinning by commission or omission?

_____

_____

_____

_____

_____

Confess and get on with it!
What else?

Too much to do?

Personally, I usually procrastinate because I've (once again) put too many pots on the stove at once and I can't decide how to cook it all. I feel overwhelmed. I cannot figure out where to start.

GRACE OVER GRIND If you are like me, instead of forging forward, stop and take a step back. Spend some time with the Lord asking Him what really takes priority. Resist moving forward until you have received an answer. This is not procrastination—it leads to assurance and clarity.

Eliminate the things that don't really need to be tackled right now. What might those things be?

_____

_____

_____

_____

_____

Then break down the impending tasks into manageable portions. When I see everything that needs to be done, I often feel overwhelmed and shut down.

But once I take a task and break it down into smaller segments, I feel like I can take on the world!

Break them down.

_____

_____

_____

_____

_____

Negativity?

Online, folks suggest that

- negative emotions and self-talk,
- fear of failure and/or success,
- believing good work = good personhood,
- focusing on the possible outcome before the process, and more...

lead to putting off what we know we should do. Do any of these resonate with you?

Let's face it, there may be as many reasons for postponing a task to reach a goal as there are numbers of us. What is your **reason**?

Change that negative message into a positive and empowering one.

Move from, I see the big task before me and feel overwhelmed to the point of shutting down to, I know once I tackle this task by breaking it into more manageable segments, I'll soar through with flying colors!

Negative Message:

_____

_____

_____

_____

_____

Positive Message:

_____

_____

_____

_____

_____

The opposite of Procrastination is ACTION.
Take action, despite distractions and procrastinations.

Here are some actionable steps:

First, figure out your own reason(s) for delaying a task.

Remember to take care of YOU.

Think positively!

Revisit your mission, vision, and goals.

Brain dump. "Mind align!" Do whatever it takes to envision the whole picture and return to your purpose once again.

Create a new "anti-dawdle" plan of action.

Break it down. Prioritize tasks.

Commit bite-sized chunks of time to the plan.

BELIEVE!

Remove distractions.

Take ACTION.

F.O.C.U.S. – Follow One Course Until Successful.

Track your progress.

Now, celebrate!

Step 25 as you PLAN PURPOSEFULLY is to remind yourself that The Opposite of Procrastination is ACTION!

Read this BLOG. Please leave a comment for us to tell us what you have learned. https://nacwe.org/2015/01/30/featured-expert-february-2015-michelle-prince-busy-busy-stop-juggling-overcome-procrastination-get-done-less-time/ https://nacwe.org/2011/06/17/4-ways-to-end-procrastination/ https://nacwe.org/2013/03/21/procrastination-three-tips-to-help-you-move-past-it/

26

STRIVE FOR THOROUGHNESS, NOT PERFECTION

Be conscientious.

"Whatever you do, work heartily, as for the Lord and not for men,..."
(Colossians 3:23)

Perfectionism is the inability or unwillingness to accept anything, any work that is less than perfect, impeccable, or flawless. It is usually rooted in fear—fear of failure and/or fear of success. Either way, perfectionism is intricately linked to procrastination because both keep you from moving forward.

I don't know about you, but ALL my coaches have impressed upon me the necessity of getting my work out there instead of procrastinating due to perfectionism.

I am going to approach this from a *Yes*, *And* perspective.

Yes – Be diligent and precise, and complete as many projects as you can. Get your work out there before perfectionism prevents any work getting out there at all.

And – Don't be careless. Don't put something out there before it is time lest you make a promise and are unable to keep it, thereby damaging your reputation for good work.

What's Your *YES*?

_____

_____

_____

What's Your *AND?*

_____

_____

_____

Accept progress over perfectionism.

"Commit your work to the Lord, and your plans will be established."
(Proverbs 16:3)

Overcoming perfectionism means you must accept progress over perfection.

Plan for it. Come up with some ways you can talk/walk yourself through the immobility caused by hair-splitting meticulousness.

List some things you can do that will help:

- Define what progress means to you.
- List the tasks necessary to get you back on track.
- Break each task down into do-able or manageable steps.

What else can you think of?

_____

_____

_____

_____

_____

Ask for help.

It often helps to have a partner or team member who can help you move through this stuckness; and it <u>can</u> be sticky. For some, this might look like hiring a virtual assistant to create graphics, proofread, and post your blogs. There are ways to work through the things you get stuck on regarding perfectionism. Just having another encouraging voice in your ear and/or an extra creative hand on the project will be a huge help.

List some folks you can call on for help:

- _____

- _____

- _____

- _____

- _____

- _____

Step 26 as you PLAN PURPOSEFULLY is Strive for Thoroughness, not Perfectionism.

Read this BLOG. Please leave a comment for us to tell us what you have learned.
https://nacwe.org/2014/10/29/struggle-perfectionism/
https://nacwe.org/2011/02/22/tips-tools-perfectionist-paralysis/

PART III
PROGRESS ALONG THE PLAN PATH
RESOURCES

Join Our Pomodoro WORK Sessions

In NACWE, we get together online Monday through Thursday at 9am CST for 2.5 hours to do a Pomodoro-type session together. We share our goals and prayer requests for the day. It is a great way to partner with like-minded women and gets things done. Join us for Pomodoro sessions following this link:

You should **join us** because everyone who shows up is really cranking out the work and making things happen.

NACWE Pomodoro Work Sessions
Monday, Tuesday, Wednesday &/or Thursdays—you choose.
9:00–11:30 AM CST
https://goo.gl/r32zu3

Work Together to form a Purposeful Plan, Design a Marketable Launch, and Follow Through to Completion.

This is what we do as a small Mastermind group when we work through C. J. Hayden's Get Clients NOW program each quarter.
We call our Program the *PDF² Program* – we Plan, Design and Follow through.

Webpage
http://karenbourg.com/PlanDesignFollowThrough

Facebook Group
By Invitation
https://www.facebook.com/groups/PlanDesignFollowThrough/

or

Join us on one of our Quarterly Writing Retreats
http://karenbourg.com/RetreattoWrite

YOU DO NOT HAVE TO DO THIS ALONE!

My Prayer for You

You Love Righteousness in Our/Your Marketplace.
You mention fairness in dealing in the marketplace and You mention numbers and counting things all through Your Word. We believe You are very interested in our check boxes.

Grant us favor in all our work and may it all lead others closer to You and cause people to praise YOU!

You Want to See Us Prosper.
...Be strong, and show yourself..., and keep the charge of the Lord your God, walking in His ways and keeping His statutes, His commandments, His rules, and His testimonies, as it is written in the Law of Moses, that you may prosper in all that you do and wherever you turn...
1 Kings 2:2-3 (David to his son) ***

You Plant Your Dreams and Desires Within Us.
You planted this dream, this vision, and You guided us thus far through this plan. Give us strength and success in the tasks before us.

You Love Kingdom Collaborations.
For where two or three are gathered in Your name, there am I among them."
(Matthew 18:20)

Lord, we ask You to bless us and our efforts to work diligently toward the plans You have set before us. Bless us when we partner together to encourage one another and pray for one another and work together.

You Want Us to Be Your Vessels in the Lives of Others.
Thank You for the reminder that You chose us to do good work, to influence others in ways that lead people to glorify You, to make a commitment and stick to it as workmen unashamed, to hope, to write out our dreams and goals, and to receive from and give encouragement to others.

Help us to take every thought captive when we begin to feel stuck, fade, and lose hope.

<u>You Desire Commitment and Confidence in Our/Your Work.</u>
You tell us to commit and do our work as if we are doing it for You. And You promise to help us establish our plans. Help us to set aside our fears and do what You have called us to do with confidence.

In Jesus' Holy Name we pray, Amen.

Blessings,
Karen

PART IV

PRAISES

27

REST IS THE SECRET TO YOUR SUCCESS

Rest? Me?

I am NEVER Still or at rest. Well, that's not entirely true, BUT it FEELS TRUE!

I have been to numerous conferences and seminars and retreats and almost every time I attend or present, someone walks up to me and tells me they arrived feeling anxious or stressed, but my calm presence helped them to relax. Honestly, most of the time I feel like a duck skimming along on a still pond—on the surface I seem to be effortlessly gliding along, but underneath I'm pedaling as fast and furiously as I can. And while there is a smile on my face, I can be miles away worrying about the next step or what will happen tomorrow. Being still and at rest is not my strong suit!

I Googled "rest for entrepreneurs" and never found the end of the articles written to encourage us to relax and take time off. In our Mastermind Group, we just went through Shae Bynes' book, *Grace Over Grind, How Grace Will Take Your Business Where Grinding Can't*, where she talks about this very thing.

She says, "In the world of entrepreneurship, hustling and grinding will earn you a badge of honor. In the Kingdom of God, it is an inferior substitute for working by the supernatural power of God's grace."

A pastor once told us that to work frantically was to resist the grace God has for us. I definitely **Do Not** want to hinder His Grace in any way!

Busy and successful are not synonyms.

According to Joseph Bienvenu, a psychiatrist and director of the Anxiety Disorders Clinic at Johns Hopkins Hospital, busyness has become a widespread health issue. He says, "Emotional distress due to overbusyness manifests as difficulty focusing and concentrating, impatience and irritability, trouble getting adequate sleep, and mental and physical fatigue." [johnshopkinshealthreview.com]

Looks like a vicious cycle to me! In contrast, when we know how to balance work with restorative rest, our productivity can skyrocket. **I am ALL IN!**

Different Types of Rest:

I read online in many places that there are different types of rest. Who knew!?

Passive Rest encompasses those quiet, contemplative times when your body, soul (mind, will and emotions), and spirit are still and being restored.

Active Rest includes engaging in physical activity and hobbies that may demand the expending of energy, but in turn give you oomph and restore you.

Social Rest requires getting out with family and/or friends for some fun relaxing and restoring relationships – away from the grind.

Rest can be physical/sensory, emotional/mental, intellectual/creative, environmental, social, and spiritual.

Choose them all.

Choose Restorative Rest.

It is a choice. It leads to productivity. One of our NACWE Team members purposefully schedules a *daily downtime* on her calendar for an hour during which time she may nap, read, meditate, pray or just be still and think. It is a short time for refreshing each day. Try it! Do you want to be busy—or do you want to make an impact? What do you need to do to rest restoratively?

Rest Restoratively

- Take regular breaks throughout the day. Short rests can significantly improve the quality of your work.
- Establish *think time* – John Maxwell says he has a thinking chair, and that is all it is used for – being still and thinking. Microsoft founder Bill Gates took time alone for "Think Weeks" – seven days spent reading, strategizing and reflecting!
- Put downtime on your calendar to prevent fatigue, reestablish priorities, restore motivation, increase creative and productive flow, AND improve your health and wellness!
- Veg-out!
- Go for walks – restorative activities can be just as helpful as literal "down" time.
- Give yourself a periodic [daily, weekly, monthly, quarterly, annual] "technology break."
- **Work to live, instead of living to work.** https://www.entrepreneur.com/article/325224

What can you add?

_____

_____

_____

_____

_____

Sticking to a 90-day plan requires focus and concentration. It takes determination and motivation. You need perseverance. The process can be both invigorating and tiring.

Rest must be a pivotal part of your plan.

It is essential to purposefully plan rest into your week. Rest for you may mean keeping your work to the working week and protecting the weekend for rest, play, and family. Rest is as important as play when it comes to giving your brain a break and revving up your creativity.

Step 27 as you PLAN PURPOSEFULLY is to Rest for Restoration—It is the Secret to Your Success.

I can't believe I'm saying this, but DON'T look at us (or them) online for a full 24–hours.

Then, come back and dive into your plan!

Read this BLOG. Please leave a comment for us to tell us what you have learned. https://karenbourg.com/2020/01/25/hurry-up-and-slow-down-in-2020/ https://karenbourg.com/2020/02/05/7-ways-to-quest-after-god/

28

PLAY! AND PLAY SOME MORE!

All Work and No Play

"All work and no play makes Jack a dull boy" is a popular saying. Who said this? It means that without time off from work, a person becomes both bored and boring. The exact origins of the phrase remain unclear, though it was recorded as early as 1659.

I am notorious for not getting started because I'm overwhelmed with the big picture.

I am notorious for finally getting started, not knowing when to stop once I'm on a roll, then quickly burning out.

I tend to think if I'm not working or engaged somehow, I am wasting time.

What about you? What is your pattern? ...and..."How's that working for ya?"

Balance

I guess we are looking for a bit of balance here.

Part of finding this balance during your Purposeful Planning spree is deciding when to work and when to play and putting BOTH on your schedule—and following that schedule!

Play (free time or fun) is an important part of rest, relaxation, refreshing, creativity, and learning. Play engages different parts of your brain. It engages different parts of your body and energy. Your playtime does not have to be strenuous, but it needs to include time <u>away</u> from your work. It needs to encompass something you find fun and pleasurable. It needs to be something that recharges YOU!

Put it on your schedule and do not compromise. You will be grateful.

Journal through some Play Quotes

Play Quotes from https://www.museumofplay.org/education/education-and-play-resources/play-quotes

I have chosen a few of my favorites.

	Journal through some Play Quotes
It is a happy talent to know how to play. *Ralph Waldo Emerson, American writer 1803–1882*	
The true object of all human life is play. *G. K. Chesterton, British author 1874–1936*	
Almost all creativity involves purposeful play. *Abraham Maslow, American psychologist 1908–1970*	
Play gives children a chance to practice what they are learning. *Fred Rogers, American television personality 1928–2003*	
Surely all God's people...like to play. *John Muir, American naturalist 1838–1914*	
Creative people are curious, flexible, persistent, and independent with a tremendous spirit of adventure and a love of play. *Henri Matisse, French painter 1869–1954*	

A child who does not play is not a child, but the man who does not play has lost forever the child who lived in him. Pablo Neruda, Chilean poet 1904–1973

Apparently,

Play can be a very praise-worthy activity!

And the streets of the city shall be full of boys and girls playing in its streets. Zechariah 8:5 (ESV)

Praise the LORD! Praise God in his sanctuary; praise him in his mighty heavens! Praise him for his mighty deeds; praise him according to his excellent greatness! Praise him with trumpet sound; praise him with lute and harp! Praise him with tambourine and dance; praise him with strings and pipe! Praise him with sounding cymbals; praise him with loud clashing cymbals! ... Psalm 150:1-6 (ESV)

Step 28 as you PLAN PURPOSEFULLY is to PLAY! And Play Some More!

Read this BLOG. Please leave a comment for us to tell us what you have learned. https://nacwe.org/2011/04/12/ask-diane-are-you-all-work-no-play/ https://nacwe.org/2010/11/24/guest-blog-finding-balance-by-desirae-shawn/

29

CELEBRATE, CONGRATULATE, & RECEIVE A REWARD

Let's talk about Celebrations, Congratulations, and Rewards.

Most of us skip the celebration part of accomplishing a goal or completing a difficult task.

Rewarding yourself is part of keeping up motivation and celebrating your keen effort.

We are so sincere about and committed to this in the National Association of Christian Women Entrepreneurs groups that we set aside time at the end of each month AND the whole month of December to celebrate Christ and to celebrate our wins and successes.

What celebration activities are most meaningful to you?

God tells us there is "a time to weep, and a time to **laugh**; a time to mourn, and a time to **dance**;... Also, that **everyone should eat and drink and take pleasure in all his toil**—this is God's gift to man." Ecclesiastes 3:4,13

(**Bold** = mine)

Celebrate! Some celebrations and rewards need to be tangible, touchable!

- Send it to the publisher.
- Take time off.
- Shout out about your accomplishment on social media (that's right; no one else is going to toot your horn for you). Toot away!
- Plan the next biggie.
- Throw a party!

How do you like to celebrate?

_____

_____

_____

_____

_____

What rewards are most motivating for you?
The type of rewards you set up for yourself do not have to be big or extravagant (but don't limit yourself, either). A reward could include

- a book signing party;
- an outing with the family;
- a trip to the bookstore by yourself;
- a purchase – I might reward myself with that new course content creation program I've been looking at;
- A gift from me to me!

What rewards do you prefer?

_____

_____

_____

_____

_____

Be creative with rewarding yourself and celebrating your accomplishments. Even little things done with the purpose and intention of reward will provide a desired effect on your spirit and mind.
Step 29 as you PLAN PURPOSEFULLY is Celebrate, Congratulate & Receive a Reward.
Read this BLOG. Please leave a comment for us to tell us what you have learned.
https://nacwe.org/2020/01/19/celebrate-2020-with-nacwe/
https://nacwe.org/2013/01/31/the-un-glamorous-ridiculously-obvious-secret-to-achieving-any-goal/

PART IV
Praises
Resources

My Prayer for you

You Offer Us Restorative Rest.
You say, *Come to me, all who labor and are heavy laden, and I will give you rest. Take my yoke upon you, and learn from me, for I am gentle and lowly in heart, and you will find rest for your souls. For my yoke is easy, and my burden is light.* Matthew 11:28-30; and *Come away by yourselves to a desolate place and rest a while.* Mark 6:31

Help us to remember that rest is restorative, and we will be more creative and successful when we take care of ourselves this way.

You Give Us Strength Even to Play.
You talk about children playing and You talk a lot about resting in Your Word. We are not going to be any heavenly good if we are earthly burned out. Give us strength. Give us rest. And may our restful and playful times restore us to do what You have called us to do.

You Encourage Us to Celebrate.
You encourage us to celebrate first by praising YOU (*Praise the Lord!* Psalm 150:1-6), then by rejoicing in the day (*This is the day that the Lord has made; let us rejoice and be glad in it.* Psalm 118:24), and with laughing and dancing (Ecclesiastes 3:4). Thank You for the reminder that all we accomplish is from You and is worth celebrating and rewarding. **May I have this dance?**

In Jesus' Holy Name we pray, Amen.

Blessings,
Karen

PART V

PLAN AGAIN

30

SHAMPOO. RINSE. REPEAT.

Shampoo. Rinse. Repeat.
Repeat. Repeat. Repeat!

When working through your 12-week plans, keep in mind what worked and works for <u>you</u>. Those are the actions you want to repeat—just as if you were doing a second shampoo during a shower. Shampoo. Rinse. Repeat! It may take a little trial and error to get your individualized and near-perfect 12-week plan together.

Stay flexible with the things that are not working and try something new right away and/or when you reset your plan for the next 12 weeks. Don't be afraid to change something mid-stream if it is counterproductive.

You won't follow your plan well or repeat actions often—even actions that do work for you—or enjoy the process and repeat it later if the actions you choose don't fit with your temperament or bring the results you desire.

Redesign a list of actions that will work for you within the reality of a 12-week plan for your personal and business goals. Then hang in there! Sticking with something for 90 days will give you a good indication of whether it is a good path for you or not.

What actions need to be abandoned?

- _____
- _____
- _____
- _____
- _____

What actions need to be retained?

- _____
- _____

- _____
- _____
- _____

What actions fit best with your style?

Not sure what steps and plans are best for you based on your own T.A.L.E.N.T.S.?

Check out Angela Hallford's T.A.L.E.N.T.S. program at http://furthermoreliving.com. It is one of the most well-rounded offerings I've found. You will explore your God-given temperament, ambitions, leadership abilities/styles, experiences, needs, talents, and spiritual gifts all in one course. In my humble opinion the combined DISC and Spiritual Gifts Assessments she walked me through were the most valuable in my career.

As a step further, C. J. Hayden's book, *Get Clients Now (™): A 28-Day Marketing Program for Professionals, Consultants, and Coaches,* is the best walk-you-through-every-step guide to develop a marketing plan for your business/ministry based on what you LOVE to do instead of what you don't. I love that approach, and it has worked very well for me EVERY time I have tried it, even when admittedly, my effort wasn't 100%. Now that is saying somethin'!

What do you know about your style, temperaments, and gifts that will ultimately help you succeed?

- _____
- _____
- _____
- _____
- _____

Bottom line: repeat what works and change what doesn't.

You will find your groove!
PLAN again ahead of time for every year and especially for every 12-week quarter. Step 30 as you PLAN PURPOSEFULLY is Shampoo. Rinse. **Repeat!**

Read this BLOG. Please leave a comment for us to tell us what you have learned. https://nacwe.org/2014/02/24/lessons-leadership-day-1-40-surrender/

31

ROUTINES AND HABITS

Best Practices Become Regular Routines

You started with best practices – The applications or uses of an idea, belief, or method, as opposed to theories relating to it.

If you perform an activity or exercise a skill repeatedly or regularly to improve or maintain your proficiency, you will develop best habits.

To succeed you must carry out or perform an activity, method, or custom regularly or habitually.

Let's DO this!

Remember, your best ways and efficient and effective systems require a lot of practice. They are the to-dos and tasks that you perform on a regular basis. They are the tasks that help you achieve your goals in the long term. Without these ongoing practices, you will not see your dreams come true.

You have developed some priorities throughout this plan that, when broken down into smaller tasks and to-dos, helped you adopt things that are now recurring and essential practices, routines and eventually habits.

You have established best practices for your day, week, month, quarter, etc. Your next 12-weeks is planned down to the daily activities you will need to tackle to accomplish your biggest dreams and visions. Hopefully, this has led you to establish routines that work for YOU. Gratefully, these routines will become established habits once you have begun to implement them.

What habits have you established or are you developing so far?

- _____

- _____

- _____

- _____
- _____

Regular Routines Become Established Habits

You have adopted routines, sequences of actions regularly followed, a fixed program (but not TOO fixed, mind you—be flexible).

The Lord is noticeably clear in Ephesians 4 and Colossians 3 that we are to put off certain things. He makes that challenging step easier when He tells us what to put on. Routinely evaluating your 12-week plan will help you determine tasks that need to be removed, added, and/or adjusted for your greatest enjoyment and highest success. (Yes—doing what God has called you to do is supposed to be fun!). Now, stick to your planned routine. Put it on your calendar!

What routine or habit needs to be placed on your calendar?

- _____
- _____
- _____
- _____
- _____

Good Habits are Hard to Give Up & Lead to Success!

Look forward to working through this proven and effective Purposeful Plan so that your practices and routines become established, settled, or regular tendencies or practices, especially ones that are hard to give up.

Your practices, routines, and habits will ensure you move closer to your goals and accomplish everything within your Purposeful Plan.

Step 31 as you PLAN PURPOSEFULLY is to establish Routines and Habits.

Read this BLOG. Please leave a comment for us to tell us what you have learned. https://karenbourg.com/2020/03/04/how-to-get-motivated-about-your-business/

My Prayer for You

<u>You Have NOT Re-Called the Calling you Have Placed on Our Lives</u>.
Thank You for the many reminders that we must grow and serve according to our God-given temperaments, ambitions, leadership abilities, experiences, needs, talents, and spiritual gifts. Help us to keep doing what You have called us to do in line with the gifts You've given us.

Serenity Prayer

*God grant me the serenity
to accept the things I cannot change;
courage to change the things I can;
and wisdom to know the difference.*

*Living one day at a time;
enjoying one moment at a time;
accepting hardships as the pathway to peace;
taking, as He did, this sinful world
as it is, not as I would have it;
trusting that He will make all things right
if I surrender to His Will;
that I may be reasonably happy in this life
and supremely happy with Him
forever in the next.*

Amen.

https://www.beliefnet.com/prayers/protestant/addiction/serenity-prayer.aspx

Do not be conformed to this world, but be transformed by the renewal of your mind, that by testing you may discern what is the will of God, what is good and acceptable and perfect. Romans 12:2

<u>You Help Us Plan according to Your Design and Will</u>.
Lord, help us to establish practices, routines, and finally habits that You would call acceptable and perfect! May all we Purposefully Plan for this 12-week session be pleasing to You and serve to draw others closer to You in their lives and businesses and ministries!

In Jesus's Holy Name we pray, Amen.

**Blessings,
Karen**

"Your God-given calling has not changed; has not been recalled, even or especially during these uncertain times!"
Let's rediscover your calling with intention!

– Karen Lindwall-Bourg

(Written as we "sheltered-in-place" – April 2020)

PART V
Plan Again
Resources

REVIEW AND REVISE

Review and Revise

Throughout the next 12-week period, you have a wonderful opportunity to continually review and revise your plan.

No judgement!

Just throw out the tasks you designed that didn't fit your personality and strengths and didn't seem to take your plan in the direction you envisioned.

Make a special note of the practices and tasks that worked well for you and advanced your plan toward completion. Make sure these are part of your continued plan and move them forward to your next 12-week plan.

Plan parts that need to be eliminated:

- For me, cold calling. I schedule it, but I rarely do it. (The introvert in me, I guess!).
- For you?

- _____

- _____

- _____

- _____

- _____

Plan segments that need to be <u>added</u>:

- For me, well-defined boundaries. (I realize if I don't want to be interrupted, I should work less at home and carve out more time in the private office where I am less distracted. AND I often disregard my own boundaries to the detriment of my client's and my own goals.)
- For you?

- _____

- _____

- _____

- _____

- Plan elements that need to be changed or **tweaked**!
- For me, I usually include way too many practices and need to focus in on the ones that are most useful and eliminate a few others.
- For you?

- _____

- _____

- _____

- _____

- _____

Plan practices that work <u>best</u> for you:

- The daily practice of tracking works well for me. (I use a simple Excel file.)
- For you?

- _____

- _____

- _____

- _____

- _____

Be Intentional About Growth.

The review involves looking at the facts and seeing what needs to be re-thought and re-designed. This is not a time to judge your performance. It is simply about reviewing and getting ready to set up your next 12 weeks. Keep your thoughts positive, and remember you are doing this again in the next quarter—and doing it better every time!

Be intentional! Growth doesn't just happen. You must plan to feed yourself to increase and succeed in all areas of your life—physically, emotionally, occupationally, intellectually, environmentally, socially, and spiritually. INVEST in yourself and in your Purposeful Plan. Part of a good plan includes scheduling and being intentional about change and growth.

What next steps do you need to take toward growth, especially as you grow your business/ministry as God has called you to it?

_____

_____

_____

_____

_____

God Bless You!

My Prayer for You

You Lead our Revisions.
Lord, Change and Growth are sometimes painful and frightening experiences. And yet they are so necessary. Guide us with Your Loving Hand as we work through this plan and these daily practices toward visions and goals that You have planted deep within our hearts. May all our plans and the changes we make to our plans be ordered by You and blessed by You.

In Jesus's Holy Name we pray, Amen.

Blessings,
Karen

Finale

PRAISES, CELEBRATIONS AND REWARDS!

Praise the Lord!

Delight yourself in the Lord,
and he will give you the desires of your heart.

Commit your way to the Lord;
trust in him, and he will act.

He will bring forth your righteousness as the light,
and your justice as the noonday. Psalm 37:4-6

You cannot do anything but for the grace of God. He gives you each breath you breathe. He puts His desires within your heart. He gives you the power to work well and to gain wealth. An attitude of thankfulness and praise every day can change your outlook and alter your success.

Invite God in to every plan, every daily practice before you begin. Praise the Lord for every task you complete and every day you finish. Take the time at the end of the quarter to look back at all you have accomplished—both big and little things—and PRAISE the LORD!

Write your PRAISE to the Lord here:

_____

_____

_____

_____

_____

Celebrate!

"...everyone should eat and drink and take pleasure in all his toil—this is God's gift to man." Ecclesiastes 3:13

Celebrate!

I always tell Christian Entrepreneurs in my groups it is okay to shout from the rooftops why you do what you do, what you do, and when you win. No one else is going to do it for you! I know we are taught not to be boastful or prideful, but that does not mean we are not supposed to be proud of the good work we have done. So, go ahead and shout it from the (virtual) rooftops!

Consider the Parable of the Talents

The Parable of the Talents – Matthew 25

*14 For it will be like a man going on a journey, who called his servants and entrusted to them his property. 15 To one he gave five talents, to another two, to another one, to each according to his ability. Then he went away. 16 He who had received the five talents went at once and traded with them, and he made five talents more. 17 So also he who had the two talents made two talents more. 18 But he who had received the one talent went and dug in the ground and hid his master's money. 19 Now after a long time the master of those servants came and settled accounts with them. 20 And he who had received the five talents came forward, bringing five talents more, saying, "Master, you delivered to me five talents; here, I have made five talents more." 21 His master said to him, **"Well done, good and faithful servant.** You have been faithful over a little; I will set you over much. **Enter into the joy of your master."** 22 And he also who had the two talents came forward, saying, "Master, you delivered to me two talents; here, I have made two talents more." 23 His master said to him, **"Well done, good and faithful servant.** You have been faithful over a little; I will set you over much. **Enter into the joy of your master."** 24 He also who had received the one talent came forward, saying, "Master, I knew you to be a hard man, reaping where you did not sow, and gathering where you scattered no seed, 25 so I was afraid, and I went and hid your talent in the ground. Here, you have what is yours." 26 But his master answered him, "You wicked and slothful servant! You knew that I reap where I have not sown and gather where I scattered no seed? 27 Then you ought to have invested my money with the bankers, and at my coming I should have received what was my own with interest. 28 So take the talent from him and give it* *to him who has the ten talents. **29** For to everyone who has will more be given, and he will have an abundance. But from the one who has not, even what he has will be taken away. **30** And cast the worthless servant into the outer darkness. In that place there will be weeping and gnashing of teeth.*

I want to hear the Master say, **"Well done, good and faithful servant."** The Lord cares about our stewardship and our accomplishments enough to celebrate with us and to reward us. ***So, should we.***

Write a declaration of celebration here:

_____

_____

_____

_____

_____

_____

_____

If you continue reading in Matthew 25, you read about the Final Judgement and the Final Reward.

Reward Yourself for a Job Well Done!

The Final Judgment and Reward – Matthew 25

31 *When the Son of Man comes in his glory, and all the angels with him, then he will sit on his glorious throne. **32** Before him will be gathered all the nations, and he will separate people one from another as a shepherd separates the sheep from the goats. **33** And he will place the sheep on his right, but the goats on the left. **34** Then the King will say to those on his right, "Come, you who are blessed by my Father, inherit the kingdom prepared for you from the foundation of the world. **35** For I was hungry and you gave me food, I was thirsty and you gave me drink, I was a stranger and you welcomed me, **36** I was naked and you clothed me, I was sick and you visited me, I was in prison and you came to me." **37** Then the righteous will answer him, saying, "Lord, when did we see you hungry and feed you, or thirsty and give you drink? **38** And when did we see you a stranger and welcome you, or naked and clothe you? **39***

And when did we see you sick or in prison and visit you?" **40** *And the King will answer them, "Truly, I say to you, as you did it to one of the least of these my brothers, you did it to me."*

*... **46** ... but the righteous [will go] into eternal life.*

SO, grant yourself and your team a reward. You deserve it! You've worked hard!

Wish-List some possible rewards:

- _____
- _____
- _____
- _____
- _____

My Prayer for You

You Love Praise and you Love to Praise Us!

Lord,

You ask us to praise You, You tell us to celebrate, and You reward us when we are faithful. Thank You for being All Present, All Knowing, and All Powerful in our lives. Thank You for guiding us through this Purposeful Planning Workbook. Thank You for ordering our steps throughout this PLAN. Thank you for fellow Christian Entrepreneurs who build supportive community and serve others as You have called them to. Bless these plans. We want to hear You say, "Well done, good and faithful servant!"

In Jesus's Holy Name we pray, Amen

CONCLUSION

I hope you've enjoyed this planning process.

I hope you've purposed to **invite God in**to the plan, to plan well, and to implement this God-given plan to the best of your ability!

WORKSHEETS & TEMPLATES

Join any of the NACWE (http://nacwe.org) and/or Karen Bourg (http://karenbourg.com) Programs and <u>ask</u> for the Purposeful Planning Worksheets and Templates for FREE.

9781733071062